INSIDE
LONDON

INSIDE
LONDON

DISCOVERING THE CLASSIC INTERIORS OF LONDON
JOE FRIEDMAN
PHOTOGRAPHY BY
PETER APRAHAMIAN

FOR JIM AND ISMAIL AND WITH SPECIAL
THANKS TO CHRISTIANE

Phaidon Press Limited
Regent's Wharf
All Saints Street
London N1 9PA

First published 1988
Reprinted in paperback
(revised and updated) 1998, 2000

ISBN 0 7148 3761 X

A CIP catalogue record for this book is available
from the British Library

Printed in Singapore

frontispiece
ASHBURNHAM HOUSE, WESTMINSTER
Now a part of Westminster School, the Staircase Compartment at
Ashburnham House dates from before the Great Fire of 1666, and is an
early example of the classical style revived in Great Britain by Inigo
Jones. It displays a sophisticated use of space and ornament.

CONTENTS

INTRODUCTION

In the summer of 1986 I combed the London area for six hectic weeks in search of period locations for the Merchant-Ivory's screen adaptation of E. M. Forster's novel *Maurice*. The action is set in Edwardian times and all the locations needed to date from around the turn of the century. London is an ancient city with monuments stretching back to the Roman occupation. I thought my job would be an easy one, and I was right when it came to exteriors. The 'outside' of London is remarkably unspoilt in parts. There are streets, parks, and squares which are virtually unchanged since the eighteenth century. But the same does not hold true for interiors, and I soon discovered that it is rare for any interior, especially a domestic interior, to survive unchanged for more than ten or twenty years. Even where period interiors do survive, they are hard to find, since they are generally concealed from the street and invisible to the passer-by. My first instinct was to head for the library. For days I waded through history books and guides to London. Many of these dealt with London's architecture, and some described and even illustrated a selection of historic interiors, but to my surprise none dealt specifically with this subject. Friends and colleagues offered valuable advice, but in the end there was nothing for it but to knock on doors and invite myself in. It was a nerve-racking and often frustrating experience, including several near misses and many slammed

doors. But the rewards were enormous. Behind the familiar and sometimes unprepossessing street fronts of buildings I had passed countless times before I encountered a thrilling range of unspoilt period interiors which had somehow escaped the ravages of modernization and redevelopment and which gave me a new insight into the history and character of London. By now I had caught some bug; today I cannot pass a building without peering through windows and opening doorways in the hope of finding some unknown architectural treasure. I decided to delve further. This book is the result.

Before I could begin I had to find a photographer. I wanted the book to be right up to date with original photographs showing interiors exactly as they survived. My first step therefore was to find someone who shared my enthusiasm for historic interiors; someone also who was prepared to rise at dawn and work late into the night if necessary to capture them when they were empty and unobstructed. Peter Aprahamian has been all these things. He could not have done a better job.

Greater London covers an area of some 600 square miles; there is an almost limitless range of types of interior; and although unspoilt examples are hard to find, there are many more than could possibly have been included in a book this size. This is not an exhaustive survey, but I have tried to be representative.

Most of the interiors are drawn from the centre of London, from the City, St James's, Mayfair, and Westminster, but many are located in outlying city areas, such as Brixton, Deptford and Finsbury Park as well as the suburbs and further reaches. In some cases I have come dangerously close to overstepping the boundary, and Londoners themselves may find it hard to believe that Carshalton and Charlton are really a part of the metropolis.

There is a great deal more to London's architectural heritage than a few city churches, the Houses of Parliament and Buckingham Palace. Some of the finest and most intriguing interiors in London are to be found in shops, hotels, restaurants, pubs, and cinemas – buildings often overlooked in conventional guides to London. It may seem odd that the book contains no photographs of church interiors, which are among the oldest and most important in London. However, I felt that there were far too many to choose from, enough to fill several volumes, and that the best were already well known. I wanted to get off the beaten track and break new ground, to feature interiors which had never before been published. I only wish I could have included more of the many sorts of interior which deserve greater attention, such as railway and underground stations, factory interiors, and even public lavatories (some of which have to be seen to be believed). Inevitably some of the interiors in this book will already be familiar, particularly to readers who visit historic buildings, but I hope that for the majority this will be a voyage of discovery, just as it was for me, and that even for those 'in the trade' there will be one or two surprises.

By period interiors I do not always mean interiors from the distant past. London has very few surviving interiors from before the Great Fire of 1666, and with one or two exceptions the examples I feature date from the late seventeenth century and after. Several were completed within living memory. The spectacular Art Deco barber shop at Austin Reed dates from the 1930s, the Italianate grotto at Malletts in Bond Street was built in the late 1960s, and Charles Jencks's Post-Modern mansion in Ladbroke Grove was completed as recently as 1981.

The process of selection was by no means fixed; it evolved along with the book. Looking back, however, I can see that there were certain considerations which

remained with me from the start and which guided me throughout. The first was authenticity. I was looking on the whole for interiors which were more or less unspoilt, genuine well-preserved examples of specific periods and styles. It is an uncanny experience to walk off a noisy twentieth-century high street into a shop such as Martyn's, a grocer's in Muswell Hill, North London, where virtually nothing has changed in almost a century, not even the display of merchandize; stranger still to battle through the crowds in Kensington and, mounting the steps of Linley Sambourne House, enter a Victorian time-capsule undisturbed since the 1870s. I recognize that in the end there is no such thing as a totally authentic period interior, one which survives in its original state. Almost all have at some stage been altered or restored, and the tiny number which have remained untouched naturally show their age. I leave it to others to decide whether it is better to allow a brilliantly coloured interior to turn an antique shade of brown or to opt instead for restoration. This book contains examples of both approaches. I believe that to a greater or lesser extent all have retained their original character.

If I was drawn to the genuine, I was also attracted by the fake, or if that is too strong a word, the antiquarian: interiors of one period dressed up with fragments and furniture of another. The English have always excelled at this, and London is fortunate in having several outstanding examples, among them No. 18 Folgate Street, a house in East London, where every period from the early eighteenth to the late nineteenth century is magically evoked through an artful arrangement of antique furnishings. Equally beguiling is the Bride of Denmark, a model Victorian pub in the basement of the Architectural Press in Queen Anne's Gate, which was assembled around 1949 from fragments salvaged from gin palaces destroyed in the Blitz.

I know how frustrating it can be to gaze at photographs of beautiful places with no hope of visiting them, so I have tried to include as many interiors as possible which are accessible to the public. I do not imagine that people will flock to the Bond Street jewellers, Tessiers, as they do to the Tower of London. I cannot see busloads of tourists descending on Claridge's or Hoare's Bank; but I should like to think that since many of the interiors I feature are so central and can easily be visited in passing, some might be tempted off the beaten track. (For those unsure about exact addresses, transport facilities and conditions of admission there is a gazetteer at the back which provides all the relevant information.)

Many of the interiors in this book are by well-known designers and craftsmen, such as Sir Christopher Wren, Robert Adam, and Grinling Gibbons. However, the architectural history of London is not just made up of famous names, and some of my favourite interiors are by designers and craftsmen who are largely forgotten or whose names were never recorded. I cannot say who designed the Edwardian interior of F. Cooke's eel-and-pie shop at Dalston Junction in East London, still less identify the craftsmen responsible for its tiled and mirrored walls, marble-topped tables, and stained glass windows and skylights; but to my way of thinking the interior of Cooke's is just as valuable and worthy of preservation as any documented drawing room by Adam in St James's, perhaps more so, since it is quite unique, the only one of its kind.

One of London's great strengths is its ability to absorb foreign communities and cultures. This is likewise a strength of English architecture, which has always thrived on foreign influence. The interior of No. 6 Carlton House Terrace, the home of the Royal Society, is virtually indistinguishable from that of a Quattrocento Florentine Palazzo. The state apartments at Lancaster House consciously evoke the

splendour of the Sun King's Palace at Versailles; and in the Arab Hall at Leighton House, with its Islamic tiles and lattice-work balconies and shutters, it is as if one had been transported to Cairo or Baghdad.

It is interesting, and sometimes astonishing, to see how interiors designed for one purpose have been converted to quite another; which explains why in almost every case I have grouped the interiors according to their present rather than their original function. Home House, for instance, a palatial Neo-classical mansion built for the Dowager Countess of Home by Robert Adam, is classified under Schools and Colleges, since it is occupied today by the Courtauld Institute, an art history faculty founded in the 1930s by textile millionaire and connoisseur, Samuel Courtauld. In the same way the Law Courts branch of Lloyds appears in the section on banks, although it started out in the 1880s as a restaurant and still preserves the exotic character of a late nineteenth-century banqueting hall.

Another characteristic feature of the English is their eccentricity and this too is reflected in their architecture. I can think of no better example than Lord Spencer's Room at Spencer House, an interior of the late 1750s which is currently being restored for use as an office. The chimney piece has been removed and the paintwork and gilding have been stripped from the plasterwork and panelling, but there is something undeniably dramatic about the bizarre screen of palm tree columns which were once flanked by marble blackamoors in pink togas brandishing bows and arrows. Equally outlandish is the Granada Bingo Hall in Tooting, once a cinema, which can only be described as a cross between a Gothic cathedral and a Moorish palace.

Behind a restrained conventional exterior the English sometimes conceal a Romantic nature. In the same way English architects have shown a tendency to

secrecy and understatement in the design of facades, giving little hint of the gorgeous and sometimes outrageous interiors concealed within. The contrast in London beween street-fronts and interiors can be staggering. Who could guess that behind the establishment facade of the Royal Automobile Club in Pall Mall lies a torch-lit Byzantine-style swimming-pool? How many commuters are aware that high above their heads at Liverpool Street Station, in an obscure corner of the Great Eastern Hotel, bolted-doors draw back to reveal an Egyptian-style Masonic temple with lotus-leaf columns and a zodiac ceiling?

Condition was of small importance in relation to quality and atmosphere, and in a number of cases I foreswore rather ritzy interiors in favour of others which were shabby and even ruinous. Spencer House is one example. Cromwell House is another. The seventeenth-century staircase compartment, one of the oldest in London, is down to the brickwork in parts, and the treads of the stairs have become worn and bowed, but enough survives of the extraordinary carved balustrade to warrant a photograph, and the future looks bright since after long years of neglect the house is at last being restored.

Paradoxically, neglect is sometimes preferable to certain forms of restoration, and there are one or two historic interiors in London which I left out because I felt that they had been overdone. But there does come a point when neglect amounts to vandalism and photographing hardly seems worthwhile. I felt this point had been reached at Danson Park in Bexleyheath, a once magnificent eighteenth-century villa which the local council has allowed to fall into ruin. Mercifully the building has recently been acquired by a local architect, Laurie Taylor, who with the assistance of English Heritage has set about the daunting task of restoring it. He hopes eventually to open the house to the public.

Danson Park is one of many historic buildings which are currently being restored. There is a new awareness of the value of conservation and a growing interest in architecture and, more particularly, interiors. Even so there are no grounds for complacency. Danson Park illustrates the point that it is still possible for a major listed building to be run down and wrecked by a local authority. Interiors are especially vulnerable, since they are hidden from view and are therefore difficult to monitor. Sadly also they are not always accorded the same importance as facades. One of the interiors in this book, the Empire Theatre in Hackney, is under threat and in desperate need of funds. Another, the St Pancras Hotel, stands empty and neglected. A third which was photographed for this book was destroyed before publication and had to be excluded. Several more disappeared before I could record them, notably Rayne's in Bond Street, which once boasted a suite of Regency Revival showrooms by the outstanding post-war stage designer Oliver Messel. I myself saw Messel's distinctive display cases being hauled out on to the street (where are they now I wonder?) and a team of workmen stripping the interior behind a make-shift screen of brown paper hastily pasted to the windows. Thank heavens for the Dorchester Hotel, which with greater foresight and respect has held on to what must now be the only surviving Messel interiors in London, one of which, the roof-top dining room, is featured in this book. I only hope that this is not destroyed when the interior of the hotel is refurbished next year.

In writing this book my aim has been to turn London inside out so as to reveal some of its greatest and least expected treasures. I believe these to be a vital part of the city's architectural heritage, and if in any way I have contributed to their future conservation, this modest book will have done its job.

SHOPS

BATES, ST JAMES'S

*B*INKS, a stray from the streets of St James's, waltzed into Bates' hatters *(left)* one afternoon in 1921 and was instantly adopted. He has never left. Stuffed by the management after his death in 1926, he continues to preside over business from a position of honour on the shelf. The top hat and cigar are anything but fanciful – according to legend, Binks was never seen without them.

JAMES SMITH & SON, BLOOMSBURY

*E*VERY Londoner requires an umbrella, and there is no better place to buy one than James Smith & Son *(above)*. Founded in 1830, the shop moved to its present premises, a former dairy, in 1856 and little besides the stock has changed in the interim. Inside and out, Smith & Son is one of the sights of London.

HARRODS, KNIGHTSBRIDGE

*T*HE only serious rival to Allen's is the splendid Edwardian Meat Hall at Harrods *(left)*, a glittering tiled interior decorated with hunting scenes and peacocks. The interior dates from 1901–3, when the famous Brompton Road facade was erected.

R. ALLEN, MAYFAIR

*T*HE original owner had to fight a legal battle for the right to hang his wares in public. But it was worth it. At Allen's in Mount Street *(left)* merchandizing has been raised to the level of a fine art, the staff take as much trouble over the daily hang of meat as any artist composing a still life. The interior is more or less as it was when the shop first opened in 1887, with colourful glazed tiles and an oak counter surmounted by hunting trophies.

W. MARTYN'S MUSWELL HILL

*L*OCALS refer to Martyn's *(right)* as 'the Fortnum and Mason of Muswell Hill'. If only Fortnum's was as well preserved. The interior of Martyn's is virtually unchanged since the owner's great-grandfather started the business in 1897. Even the display of merchandize is in period. Particularly impressive are the display cases with finely wrought barley-twist colonettes.

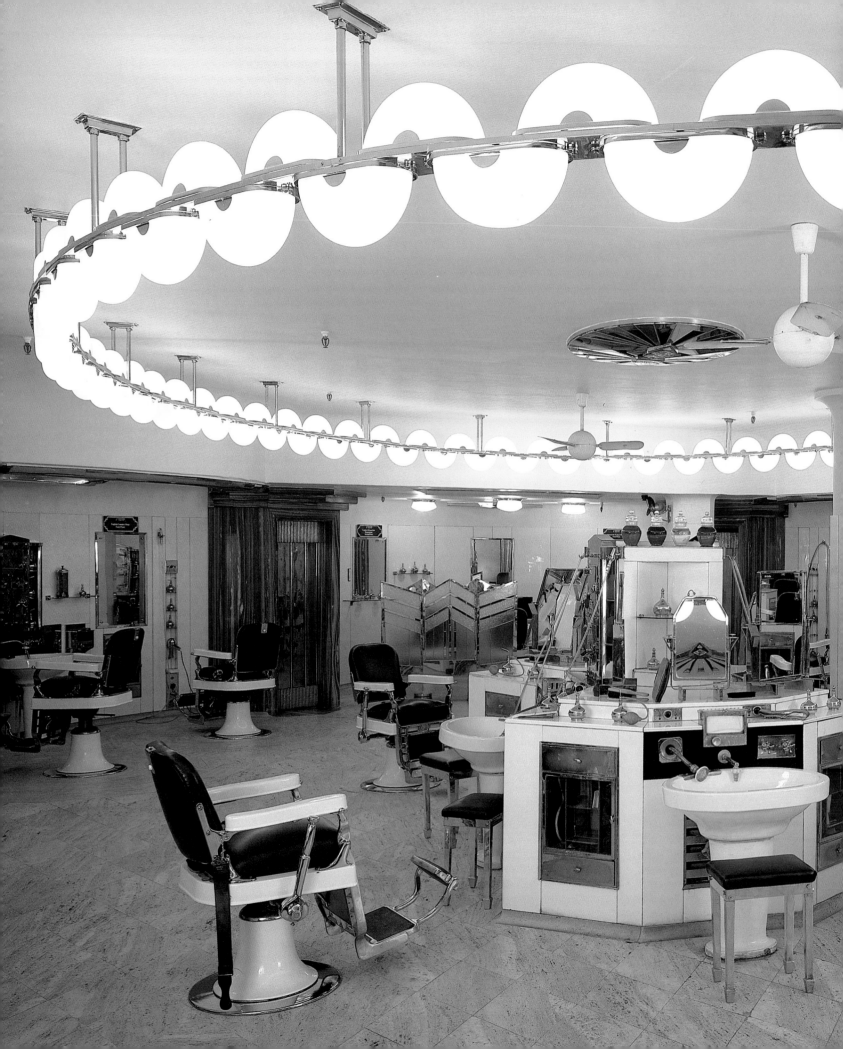

AUSTIN REED,
REGENT STREET

*C*ONCEALED behind a sedate
Edwardian facade, the Art Deco
Barber Shop at Austin Reed is
one of the great secrets of
Regent Street. Oval in form,
with a continuous wave-scroll
ceiling light, it preserves its
original basins and chairs,
together with striking chevron
screens in chrome and frosted
glass. The floor is of Travertine
marble, the walls of pale blue
vitrolite. Altogether the most
complete interior of its kind in
London.

BERRY BROTHERS, ST JAMES'S

BERRY Brothers *(above)* have been in business for over three hundred years and are still a family concern, best known for their excellent clarets and the Cutty Sark brand of whisky. The shop was built in the 1730s and stands on the site of a late seventeenth-century coffee shop, whose original painted sign still hangs outside. The floor dips alarmingly in parts and the walls are lined with antique letters.

Since 1765 the scales on the right have been used to weigh celebrities, and nine leather-bound volumes contain the facts on such distinguished former customers as the poet Byron and Napoleon III.

TESSIERS, BOND STREET

TESSIERS *(right)* opened on Bond Street in 1852 but the business was founded much earlier in the eighteenth century by Lewis Tessier, the grandson of a Hugenot exile said to be descended from the Kings of Sicily. In Victorian times Tessiers were not only jewellers and silversmiths, but 'artists in hair', and examples of their work still hang above the mahogany and looking-glass display cabinets on the right. No one should be deceived by the gas mantels projecting from the mirrors. These were introduced in 1973, when an industrial dispute led to crippling power cuts which left the rest of Bond Street in darkness. Ironically this is almost the only thing at Tessiers which has changed.

MALLETTS, BOND STREET

*T*HE last thing one expects to find in a smart antique shop is a grotto, but in the minds of the management at Malletts grottoes and antiques seem strangely connected. Both their branches of business have showrooms of this kind. The first *(above)*, in Bond Street was designed by architect Raymond Erith in 1968, and is said to have been inspired by a similar interior at the Villa d'Este in Rome. The second *(right)*, at Bourden House in Davies Street, is made up almost entirely of shells and was completed as recently as 1975.

RESTAURANTS

F. COOKE, DALSTON

*T*HIS traditional eel-and-pie shop *(above and left)* is one of the great sights of London. The interior dates from around 1910 and features stained glass windows and skylights, Baroque Revival plasterwork, marble-topped tables, and tiled and mirrored walls.

CAFE ROYAL, REGENT STREET

*A*N atmosphere of sensuality and scandal still pervades the crimson and gilt interior of the Grill Room at the Café Royal *(overleaf)*, once the haunt of playwright Oscar Wilde and his circle. The interior dates from the 1860s and is among the earliest of its kind in London, featuring a Rococo Revival ceiling with inset painted panels and mirrored walls divided by caryatids supporting vases.

RULE'S, COVENT GARDEN

SAID to have been the favourite restaurant of Edward VII and his mistress Lily Langtry, Rule's is little changed since it opened in the 1890s, and the principal dining room *(left)* has immense period charm and atmosphere. Back stairs lead to private dining rooms on the upper storeys.

SAGNE'S PATISSERIE, MARYLEBONE

SAGNE'S was founded in the early 1920s by an immigrant Swiss pastry-lover, and despite several changes of ownership it retains a strong continental atmosphere. The walls are painted with classical landscapes and ruins, and a fine Pompeian-style mirror hangs opposite the door.

SIMPSONS IN THE STRAND

SIMPSONS started out as a chess club in the 1820s, but by the time the present building was erected in the 1890s it had become the 'Simpson's Grand Divan Tavern'. The ground-floor Dining Room is a baronial affair in the Arts and Crafts style, with inlaid panelling, but the first-floor is occupied by a suite of Neo-classical interiors in the style of Robert Adam. The best of these (left) has delicate lunettes set into a barrel-vaulted ceiling, pastel-green panelling, and original benches and tables.

THE CRITERION BRASSERIE, PICCADILLY CIRCUS

STEPPING into the Criterion Brasserie is like stepping into a painting by Klimt, but for years this resplendent interior lay concealed behind hardboard panels and a suspended ceiling. Now that it has been exposed and restored we can all admire the Moorish arcades and gilt mosaics, which date from Edwardian times.

RISTORANTE ITALIANO, MAYFAIR

*T*HIS unpretentious Italian restaurant occupies the
ground and first floors of a terraced house in Curzon
Street. The ground floor has been modernized but on the
first floor is a Rococo interior *(above)* which must once
have been an extremely fancy drawing room. The walls
are divided into curvilinear scrollwork panels,

ornamented with foliage and musical trophies,
reminiscent of the style in vogue in France during the
reign of Louis XV. The interior probably dates around
the time of the *Entente Cordiale* (1904), when the warmth
of Anglo-French relations brought about a revival of this
style.

HOTELS

INVERNESS COURT HOTEL, BAYSWATER

*N*OW a hotel, this Bayswater mansion was reputedly built as a love-nest for a Victorian businessman and his mistress. They obviously enjoyed a rich and varied relationship. The interiors range in style from early Georgian to Louis XVI and there is even a bar-room composed of boxes from a disused continental music hall.

Quite what the architect had in mind in the Staircase Hall *(above)* I cannot say. The gilded putti and the allegorical ceiling painting are recognizably baroque, but the stained glass windows and the richly carved balustrade might have come from some late medieval manor house. Well worth a visit.

THE SAVOY HOTEL, THE STRAND

*M*UCH of the Savoy Hotel has been remodelled and modernized. The principal rooms have been redecorated, but there are corners of the building where time appears to have stood still. The busy lobby *(left)*, linking the front and rear areas of the hotel, is almost exactly as it was when its designer Basil Ionides completed work in 1929.

The recess contains a stylish fitted bench, the terminals forming volutes, and is faced with looking-glass etched to represent a fountain. The chandelier is original, too.

CLARIDGE'S, MAYFAIR

*I*N the public rooms at Claridge's anyone who abides by house rules can enjoy the very best in Art Deco design. Meticulously maintained by the management and staff, this is the best preserved of London's historic hotels. The side entrance *(above)* is characteristic of the glamour and excellence of the decoration, supervised by Basil Ionides in the mid-1920s.

DORCHESTER HOTEL, PARK LANE

*T*HE Dining Room above is one of a suite of interiors at the
Dorchester by the outstanding post-war stage designer Oliver
Messel and was completed in 1953, Coronation Year. The room is
conceived as a temple to Bacchus, the god of wine, who presides
from a baldaquin over the chimney piece. Gilded foliage covers the
mirrored walls, and in the far right-hand corner, nearest the door,
a caged bird suggests that in Messel's imagination diners at the
Dorchester were so many birds in gilded cages.

PARK LANE HOTEL, PICCADILLY

*I*T is the easiest thing in the world to pop one's head through the
ballroom entrance of the Park Lane Hotel on Piccadilly and take in
the remarkable Jazz Age Foyer *(right)*, completed to the designs of
Henry Tanner in 1927. The interior is virtually complete, with
original murals and stylish silver-framed chairs and sofas.

THE GREAT EASTERN HOTEL, LIVERPOOL STREET STATION

A Pharaonic burial chamber? A set for *The Magic Flute*? The Freemasons' Temple *(above)* at the Great Eastern Hotel could be mistaken for both. Built in 1912, this solemn and little-known interior is still in use. When meetings are in session all the lights are extinguished except for the central star. The effect is positively eerie.

ST PANCRAS HOTEL, EUSTON

*T*HE staircase at the St Pancras Hotel *(right)* combines two great nineteenth-century passions: engineering and Gothic architecture. Completed to the designs of Sir George Gilbert Scott in 1878, it is a monumental construction in iron and stone with ochre walls stencilled in gold with fleurs de lys. For years the building has stood empty and neglected.

CLUBS AND SOCIETIES

THE REFORM CLUB, PALL MALL

*C*OMPLETED in 1841, the top-lit colonnaded Hall of the
Reform Club *(left)* is a breathtaking example of the
Italian Palazzo style, with polychromatic decoration in a
dozen different colours and materials. The club was
founded in 1836 by champions of electoral reform, but in
the course of time politics has politely been removed from
the agenda.

ROYAL SOCIETY, CARLTON HOUSE TERRACE

*T*HE Entrance Hall of the Royal Society *(above)* is
virtually indistinguishable from that of a Quattrocento
Florentine palazzo. The exquisite marble carvings and
inlaid doors might have been commissioned by Lorenzo
di Medici himself. In fact they were made around 1890
for Argentine millionaire C.H. Sandford, whose
extravagance extended to the erection of a mother-of-
pearl ceiling over the main staircase.

THE ATHENAEUM CLUB, PALL MALL

A statue of Apollo presides over the stately Grecian entrance hall of the Athenaeum Club, completed in 1830 to the designs of Decimus Burton, best known for the Ionic Screen at Hyde Park Corner. No less august is the Library *(above)* piled from floor to ceiling with rare editions in exquisite bindings.

ROYAL AUTOMOBILE CLUB, PALL MALL

*B*UILT in 1909–11 by the Anglo-French partnership of Arthur Davis and Charles Mewès, the Royal Automobile Club *(overleaf)* is a curious but typically Edwardian amalgam of different styles. The facade is Louis XV, with a backward glance at Gabriel's colonnaded buildings in the Place de la Concorde in Paris. The dining room is Louis XVI, with a wealth of late eighteenth-century French detail. But most spectacular of all is the torch-lit swimming-pool in the basement which can only be described as Byzantine. Descending the staircase one instantly feels like an extra in an epic motion picture by Cecil B. de Mille, or a classical sybarite in a suggestive painting by Alma Tadema.

TRAVELLERS' CLUB, PALL MALL

*F*OUNDED in the years after Waterloo as a meeting place for travelled English gentlemen and their distinguished foreign guests, the Travellers' Club has always been associated with a cultivated, cosmopolitan view of the world. The building was designed by Sir Charles Barry, architect of the adjoining Reform Club, *(qv)*. The facade heralded the arrival of the Italian Palazzo style, but the interior was more diverse, the Library *(left)* combines a replica of an ancient Greek frieze with Roman columnar screens grained in imitation of light oak.

BROOKS'S CLUB, ST JAMES'S

*S*CRUPULOUSLY restored after a recent fire, the great Subscription Room at Brooks's is one of the most elegant interiors in clubland. It is also one of the earliest, dating from the late 1770s and was designed by the architect Henry Holland. The simplicity and restraint of the interior, its simple geometry, and the shallow relief of the plaster decoration are typical of Neo-classical design in the generation after Robert Adam.

PUBLIC HOUSES

THE SALISBURY, HARINGAY

*T*HE decoration literally spills out on to the street from this late Victorian gin palace in north London *(left)*. Fruity tile-work porches lead through to a cavernous bar room, best seen through a dense cloud of cigarette smoke at closing time.

YE OLDE CHESHIRE CHEESE, FLEET STREET

*W*ITH its blackened walls, open fire, and bare floor boards strewn with sawdust 'Ye Olde Cheshire Cheese' *(above)* is everyone's idea of a traditional London tavern. A sign over the front door announces that the building was erected in the late seventeenth century and legend has it that Samuel Johnson was a customer, compiling his 'Dictionary' over ale and biscuits.

THE RED LION, ST JAMES'S

*T*HE interior of The Red Lion (*above*) has all the ingredients of the classic Victorian pub: etched glass, carved and polished woodwork, and a Lincrusta (embossed paper) ceiling. Sadly interiors of this sort are fast disappearing. Most of London's pubs are owned by breweries and other corporations which tend to impose a uniform house style on all their properties, often replacing genuine period fittings with vulgar reproductions.

THE BLACK FRIAR, BLACKFRIARS

*B*UILT by the architect H. Fuller Clarke in 1905, the Black Friar is a uniquely fine example of an Arts and Crafts pub. The interior is in an excellent state of preservation with grinning figures and bronze reliefs on a mock monastic theme by distinguished sculptor Henry Poole.

SEIZE OCCASION

A GOOD THING IS SOON SNATCHED UP

INDUSTRY IS ALL

THE BRIDE OF DENMARK, QUEEN ANNE'S GATE

Not so much a pub; more a private bar. The Bride of Denmark occupied a warren of basement rooms in Queen Anne's Gate (formerly home of the Architectural Press). No one should be fooled by the decoration. The interior *(above)* was assembled around 1949 from fragments of Victorian pubs destroyed during the Blitz.

DOMESTIC INTERIORS

CHARLTON HOUSE, GREENWICH

*C*HARLTON is a typical Jacobean manor house, erected in 1607–12 for Adam Newton, tutor to Prince Henry, the son of James I. The building has served a multitude of purposes – today it is used as a local community centre – and yet much of the original decoration survives intact, including the magnificent chimney piece above, carved in marble with figures of Vulcan and Venus and attributed to the sculptor Nicholas Stone.

NO. 18 FOLGATE STREET, SPITALFIELDS

AT No. 18 Folgate Street, an early eighteenth-century house in Spitalfields, East London, American Dennis Severs has succeeded resurrecting the past, magically evoking the eighteenth and nineteenth centuries through a series of antiquarian interiors decorated in every style from the reign of Queen Anne to that of Queen Victoria. Especially beguiling are the late Georgian bedroom in a glorious peach colour; the abandoned Victorian garret *(right)* hung with cobwebs and crimson velvet; and the mid-eighteenth century Dining Room *(above)* which resurrects exactly the confusion of a drunken dinner party depicted in a painting (attributed optimistically to Hogarth) over the chimney piece.

HAM HOUSE, SURREY

*E*VERYTHING survives at Ham: the architecture, the gardens, the furniture, even the archives. This has enabled the National Trust, which owns the property, and the Victoria and Albert Museum, which acts as administrator, to recreate the original appearance and atmosphere of this remarkable seventeenth-century relic. The house was built for Sir Thomas Vavasour, whipping boy to Charles I, but most of the interiors date from the 1760s when Ham was occupied by the Duke and Duchess of Lauderdale, whose bedchamber is pictured above.

SOUTHSIDE HOUSE, WIMBLEDON COMMON

*C*ONTROVERSY surrounds the interior of Southside House *(right)*, which some believe to be genuine but which may well be antiquarian, an artful combination of antique furnishings and fragments assembled in the nineteenth century. Personal favourites are the candle-lit 'Elizabethan' Dining Room and the 'Renaissance' Hall. But there are many more and since the house is sometimes open to the public, it is best to explore – and decide – for oneself.

OSTERLEY PARK HOUSE, ISLEWORTH

OSTERLEY is a sixteenth-century manor house remodelled in the second half of the eighteenth century by Robert Adam. The so-called Etruscan Room (above) is a typically eclectic fusion of ornaments derived from a variety of classical sources, including Greek vases and Pompeian wall paintings.

ORLEANS HOUSE, TWICKENHAM

THIS octagonal garden pavilion is all that remains of Orleans House (right), an eighteenth-century Thameside villa occupied between 1815–17 by Louis Philippe, Duc d'Orleans later King of France. The Octagon was designed by the distinguished English architect, James Gibbs, best known for the church of St Martin-in-the-Fields, Trafalgar Square. The decoration is in the Baroque style with virtuoso plasterwork by Italian stuccatori.

MARBLE HILL HOUSE, TWICKENHAM

THIS elegant Palladian villa, reproduced here by kind permission of English Heritage, dates from the 1720s and was built for the Countess of Suffolk, a mistress of George II. Small in scale, but exquisitely proportioned and finished, Marble Hill has all the characteristics of a doll's house. A finely carved staircase leads up to the Great Room *(above)* a perfect cube with paintings of Roman ruins by Panini, gilded plasterwork and woodwork, and a typically formal arrangement of early Georgian furniture.

SOANE MUSEUM, LINCOLNS INN FIELDS

WHEN architect Sir John Soane bequeathed his house to the nation in 1837 he did so on condition that nothing be disturbed, that the interior remain exactly as he left it. His wish has largely been fulfilled and the visitors can still experience at first hand the romantic, not to say eccentric, atmosphere of this early nineteenth-century museum house. The first-floor Drawing Room *(right)* has recently been restored to its original brilliance, with lemon-yellow paintwork and upholstery. The Breakfast Room *(overleaf)* on the ground floor is more subdued. The shallow dome with incised geometric ornaments and the use of indirect lighting are typical of Soane's work, as is the use of indirect lighting, mirrors, and the tantalizing perspectives.

THE THEMATIC HOUSE, LADBROKE GROVE

DESIGNED by the partnership of architect Terry Farrell and architectural thinker and *eminence*, Charles Jencks, this Post-modern mansion in Ladbroke Grove is a unique example of what its owner (Jencks) describes as 'radical eclecticism'

LINLEY SAMBOURNE HOUSE, KENSINGTON

LINLEY Sambourne House *(overleaf)* is far and away the most atmospheric historic house in London, a Victorian time-capsule undisturbed since the 1870s. With its Bohemian jumble of furniture and objects, its ageing paintwork and upholstery, this unique example of the 'Artistic' style of decoration has an authenticity possessed by few other historic houses anywhere in the world.

Little Holland House, Carshalton

Without the timely intervention of the local council this Arts and Crafts house would have fallen prey to a local developer and the Sitting Room *(above)* would have been converted into a garage. Instead it has been restored and opened as a public museum. Begun in 1902, Little Holland House was designed and built by self-taught artist-craftsman Frank Dickinson, a disciple of Ruskin and Morris, who lived here until his death in 1963. Everything was hand-made by Dickinson.

Leighton House, Kensington

In the Arab Hall at Leighton House, originally the home of Victorian painter Sir Frederick Leighton, it is as if one had somehow been transported to Cairo or Baghdad. The Islamic tiles are antique, some dating from the seventeenth century. When the sun streams through the lattice-work shutters and water trickles from the fountain in the centre I long to loll on the damask-covered benches and summon my hookah-pipe and belly-dancers.

STUDIO HOUSE, CHELSEA

*I*N the nineteenth century, long before
it was colonized by Sloane Rangers
and Punk Rockers, Chelsea was a community
of artists and writers, and its streets are
still lined with studio houses, one of
which has remained in the same
Bohemian family for almost a century
and is more or less unchanged. Electric
light has been introduced, bringing a
modicum of modern comfort to the
interior (note the frolicking putti
supporting light bulbs), but sputtering
gas fires threaten to reduce the place to
ashes.

THEATRES AND CINEMAS

THE LONDON COLISEUM, ST MARTIN'S LANE

*B*UILT in 1903–4 for theatrical impressario Oswald Stoll, the London Coliseum was originally a music hall but it has been occupied since 1968 by the English National Opera Company. The vast auditorium seats over 3,000 spectators, but with most eyes fixed on the stage or the audience, superb architectural details such as the lion-drawn chariot and charioteer *(above)* can sometimes be overlooked.

THE EMPIRE THEATRE, HACKNEY

*W*HEN film director Franco Zeffirelli launched his screen adaptation of Verdi's *La Traviata*, he announced that he was taking 'Opera to Texas'. Frank Matcham, the architect of the Empire Theatre, did likewise, bringing the opulent decoration of Italy's great opera houses to a music hall in Hackney *(right)*. The Empire opened in 1901 but was later acquired by the Mecca organization and converted into a Bingo Hall. It has since been acquired by a local preservation trust which is doing all it can to restore the theatre to its original use and splendour.

THE PLAYHOUSE THEATRE, EMBANKMENT

*A*FTER careful restoration, the interior of
the Playhouse is much as it was when the
theatre first opened in 1906. Its construction
involved a large contingent of French
designers and craftsmen, whose presence can
still be felt in the light-hearted Gallic
decoration of the walls and drop curtain. An
ingenious detail is the sacrificial ox skull in
the Doric frieze by the exit, which despite its
ancient classical origins has been wired as an
electric wall light.

ACADEMY THEATRE, BRIXTON

Nothing, not even the spectacular Art Deco Foyer above, prepares the visitor for the outrageous decoration of the auditorium of the Academy Theatre, Brixton. Below a ceiling painted to represent a star-lit sky, the proscenium arch and wings form an elaborate Mediterranean villa-and-garden complex, complete with statues, balconies, loggias and artificial trees and vegetation.

GRANADA BINGO HALL, TOOTING

*T*ODAY we would call it escapist, but in the
1920s and 30s the word was 'atmospheric'. Of all
the 'atmospheric' cinemas built in London at
that time, the Tooting Granada, which operates
today as a bingo club, was the most splendid.
The architect, Theodore Komisarjevsky, saw it
as his mission to supply cinema audiences with
'the flavour for romance for which they crave'.
At Tooting he certainly succeeded. The
auditorium is conceived as a medieval
Cathedral, with stained glass windows, Gothic
tracery and frescoes; the foyer evokes the
atmosphere of a baronial hall; and the Hall of
Mirrors is like something out of the Alhambra
Palace.

New Rainbow Theatre, Finsbury Park

Most of London's great cinemas have either been subdivided or converted into bingo halls. The New Rainbow Theatre (originally the Astoria) is unusual in that it serves as the headquarters of a branch of the Pentecostal Church. The decoration of the Foyer *(right)* is straight out of the *Arabian Nights*, but the atmosphere is more like 'the morning after'. The fountain in the centre is defunct, and flooding has caused serious damage to the paintwork in the dome.

Savoy Theatre, The Strand

Designed by Basil Ionides in 1929, the Savoy is the finest and best preserved Art Deco theatre in London. The auditorium retains its original carpet and cut velvet seat covers, but the most exciting interior is probably the rear entrance *(above)*, which combines a unique 'whirlpool' ceiling and a geometric inlaid marble floor with an Egyptian-style trophy and a metalwork bench ornamented with shells.

OFFICES

LICHFIELD HOUSE, ST JAMES'S

*B*UILT in the 1760s by James 'Athenian' Stuart, Lichfield House was the first terraced house in London to boast a Greek temple façade, with engaged columns copied from the Erectheion on the Acropolis. The interior was similar in style, but was overlaid in the 1790s by another architect, Samuel Wyatt, and there are parts of the building where it is hard to distinguish between the two phases of decoration. The top-lit Staircase Hall *(above)* is a case in point. Since 1856 the building has been occupied – and well maintained – by Clerical Medical Investment Group Limited.

SPENCER HOUSE, ST JAMES'S

*S*PENCER House – a Portland stone palace overlooking Green Park – was built in the mid-eighteenth century for John, 1st Earl Spencer. The interiors range from the Palladian to the Neo-classical, but no stylistic label fits Lord Spencer's Room which, with its bizarre screen of palm-tree columns, is one of London's greatest architectural curios. An analysis of the paintwork has revealed that the walls were originally green, with the frieze picked out in white and gold. The coffering in the alcove was a mixture of all these colours plus pink. The frieze is copied from the Temple of Antoninus and Faustina in Rome, an appropriate choice since its principal ornament, the griffin, is also the Spencer family device. The building has been fully restored since the taking of this photograph.

NO. 8 CLIFFORD STREET, MAYFAIR

*I*LLUSIONISTIC murals decorate the walls of this early Georgian town house which has served in its time as a tea shop and an office block. The panel on the left has been attributed to Sir James Thornhill, Serjeant Painter to George I. The awkward fit would suggest that it had been cut down and might even have been intended for a different setting.

CROMWELL HOUSE HIGHGATE

*A*FTER years of neglect, Cromwell House has been restored for use as an office building. The Staircase *(right)* is thought to date from around 1640 and may well be the earliest in London. The principal feature is the balustrade, carved with military and heraldic ornaments celebrating the achievements of the original residents.

LLOYDS REGISTER OF SHIPPING, THE CITY

*T*HE interior of Lloyds *(left)* is a curious blend of the Edwardian Baroque and the Arts and Crafts, with painted ceilings apparently inspired by Michelangelo's Sistine Chapel at the Vatican. The architect was Thomas Colcutt, the versatile designer of Simpson's-in-the-Strand (see Restaurants), and Frank Brangwyn was among the artists responsible for the decorative paintwork. Note the colossal marble and tile-work chimney piece and the futuristic chandeliers.

WILLIAM KENT HOUSE, ST JAMES'S

*D*ESIGNED by the architect William Kent, this mid-eighteenth century mansion was originally the home of Prime Minister Henry Pelham. Today it functions as the London headquarters of the Eagle Star insurance group, which has lavished millions on its restoration. Crimson damask lines the walls of the opulent Palladian Board Room *(above)*, which retains its original marble chimney piece and overmantel and its coved and coffered ceiling painted with classical figures.

Oak Room, (Thames Water Authority) Islington

*T*wice dismantled and rebuilt, this late seventeenth-century Board Room is situated today in a 1920s office building in Islington occupied by the Thames Water Authority. Originally it formed part of Cistern House, the headquarters of a company set up in 1613 to bring fresh water to London from unpolluted sources in Hertfordshire.

The carvings over the chimney piece, a detail of which is seen on the right, are by Grinling Gibbons, who collaborated with Sir Christopher Wren on the decoration of St Paul's Cathedral. The ceiling is ornamented with exuberant Baroque plasterwork and a painting representing the Apotheosis of William III. The curious object on the top right-hand shelf is a section of wooden tubing which was used to channel water before the introduction of metal piping.

FORMER DAILY MAIL OFFICES, FLEET STREET

*C*ARMELITE House, a Victorian Gothic office building off Fleet Street, was long occupied by the *Daily Mail* newspaper. The Board Room, a unique example of Napoleonic style decoration, with pedimented mahogany bookcases has been dismantled and rebuilt in their new premises, however, there was no possible way of transporting the Staircase Hall *(above)* which features an ornate ironwork balustrade, lift shaft and rare Art Nouveau morals representing allegorical figures and great men of literature.

FORMER DAILY EXPRESS OFFICES, FLEET STREET

*I*N designing the entrance hall of the former *Daily Express* building in Fleet Street the architect Robert Atkinson somehow managed to combine the form of a medieval chapter house with the metalwork finish of a spaceship. Particularly striking are the allegorical reliefs representing colonial enterprise and the chromium-plated handrail on the staircase taking the form of serpents.

BANKS

HOARE'S BANK, FLEET STREET

*T*HE Banking Hall at Hoare's *(above)* is virtually unchanged since its completion in the 1830s. Original customers would instantly recognize the magnificent oil burning stove, rising from the centre of the stone-flagged floor, capped by a classical lamp and decorated with a Greek Revival frieze of gilded honey-suckle. Protective screens have not been allowed to disfigure the beautifully finished counters, and the porters still wear period costume.

BANK OF ENGLAND, THE CITY

*T*HE Court Room (right) built in the 1700s, is all that survives of the old Bank of England, which was demolished and greatly enlarged in the 1920s and 30s by the architect Henry Baker. The room was designed by Sir Robert Taylor, and is typical of his style, combining Classical and Rococo elements. But Taylor would probably have had difficulty finding the interior, let alone identifying it, since it has been removed from its original position on the ground floor to its present location on the first and has otherwise been altered and 'improved'.

BARCLAYS BANK, PICCADILLY

ONE would never guess that the spectacular oriental-style interior of No. 160 Piccadilly (*above and right*) had been designed as a car showroom; it is hard enough to believe that it functions today as a bank. Free-standing red lacquer columns support a vaulted ceiling, while the floor is inlaid with concentric black and white stars in marble. The counters and furniture are of black and red lacquer with Chinese ornaments in gold. The oriental theme is continued in the manager's office (*right*) which could be mistaken for the counting house of some eighteenth-century trader in Canton.

LLOYDS BANK, THE STRAND

BUILT in 1883, the Law Courts Branch of Lloyds Bank was originally a restaurant and club for lawyers. Lloyds took possession in 1895, but the Entrance Hall (*overleaf*) is much as it was originally, with exotic virtuoso tilework by Doulton's. The building stands on the site of a seventeenth-century tavern called 'The Palsgrave Head' in tribute to Frederick Palsgrave, King of Bohemia, who married Elizabeth Stuart, daughter of James I. Portraits of the King and Queen appear in the decoration of the foyer, together with characters from the plays of dramatist Ben Jonson, who was a regular customer.

HOSPITALS

ROYAL HOSPITAL OF CHELSEA

*F*OUNDED in 1682 as a home for army veterans and disabled heroes, the Royal Hospital of Chelsea is London's answer to the Hôtel des Invalides in Paris. The Hall and Chapel, by Sir Christopher Wren, are familiar sights, but few visitors are allowed to see dormitories. The carpet and curtains are modern concessions to comfort and privacy, but otherwise the Long Ward *(above)* remains more or less unchanged.

GROVELANDS PRIORY HOSPITAL, SOUTHGATE

*P*ICTURED on the left is the remarkable vaulted Breakfast Room at Grosvenor Priory, an elegant Neo-classical villa built by John Nash in 1798, which has recently been converted into a private clinic. The room is painted to represent the interior of a bird cage set in an idyllic landscape. *Trompe-l'oeil* interiors of this date and style are extremely rare.

THE OLD OPERATING THEATRE, ST THOMAS'S HOSPITAL, SOUTHWARK

*T*HE operating theatre at St Thomas's Hospital *(overleaf)* dates from 1821, long before the introduction of anaesthetic, and is the oldest surviving interior of its kind in England. Remarkably the room is located in the attic of the Chapter House of Southwark Cathedral and once served as an apothecary's herb garret. It was bricked up in the mid-nineteenth century and only rediscovered in 1956. On display is a gruesome array of antique surgical instruments and a box of sawdust designed to catch the blood that dripped down from the operating table. Notice also the blood-stained apron in the corner and the sign on the far wall which reads *'Miseratione Non Mercede'* (Act out of compassion, and not for gain).

SCHOOLS AND COLLEGES

St Philomena's Convent, Carshalton

*T*HE Bathroom at Carshalton House *(above)* must be one of the earliest interiors of its kind in London. Completed in 1720, it is situated in a free-standing water tower in the grounds and it is decorated with original Delft tiles imported from Holland. Five marble steps lead down to a huge Roman-style bath measuring eight feet by eleven.

HARROW SCHOOL

COMPLETED around 1615, the Fourth Form Room at Harrow *(above)* provides a grim reminder of the rigours of education in the early seventeenth century. Originally the school took only forty boys, all of whom gathered here for lessons under the watchful eye of the Headmaster and his assistant. Over the centuries departing Harrovians have been encouraged to carve their names on the panelling and furniture, with the result that there is graffiti here by such distinguished former pupils as the poet Byron, and several Prime Ministers, including Peel and Churchill.

HOME HOUSE (FORMERLY THE COURTAULD INSTITUTE), PORTMAN SQUARE

ROBERT Adam built this palatial Neo-classical mansion in 1773–6, which was for many years occupied by the Courtauld Institute, an art history faculty founded by the textile millionaire and connoisseur Samuel Courtauld. The climax to Adam's design is the Staircase *(right)*: towering top-lit construction decorated with illusionistic murals and grisaille panels by Angelica Kauffmann and Antonio Zucchi.

STRAWBERRY HILL, TWICKENHAM

STRAWBERRY Hill is a castellated Gothic Revival villa built in the second half of the eighteenth century for wit and connoisseur Horace Walpole. The building is used today as a school, but the interior is well preserved with a wealth of Gothic detail culled from a bewildering variety of medieval sources. Revivalism in the arts, the resurrection of past styles, is something one associates with the Victorian age. Strawberry Hill shows that this fascinating phenomenon began much earlier.

THE RICHMOND FELLOWSHIP, HOLLAND PARK

BY the turn of the twentieth century the construction of grand houses in London had passed out of the hands of the aristocracy and into those of wealthy middle-class businessmen. This town house of 1905–06 with its peacock-coloured decoration, was originally the home of department store millionaire Sir Ernest Debenham. Debenham's architect was Halsey Ricardo, but the Domed Hall *(right)* was largely the work of Gaetano Meo, and George Jack, who added the Byzantine-style mosaic ceiling and balconies in 1913. The tiles are original and produced by William de Morgan. Some are reputed to have come from the Tzar of Russia's yacht, *Livadia*.

GOVERNMENT AND CIVIC BUILDINGS

DEPTFORD TOWN HALL

*A*FTER an absence of almost two hundred years the Baroque style returns to London and flowers as never before in the giddy-making Staircase Hall of Deptford Town Hall *(left)*, built to the designs of architect Charles E. Rickards in 1902–05. The mermaids flanking the entrance to the Council Chamber are a reminder of Deptford's ties with the port of London. Only the lantern seems out of place, an inverted umbrella which might have come from Brighton Pavilion.

WESTMINSTER HALL

*W*ESTMINSTER Hall is one of London's oldest surviving interiors. The foundations and lower portions of the walls are Norman and date from the end of the eleventh century. The masonry and carpentry *(above)* are the work of Henry Yvele and Hugh Herland and were added in the reign of Richard II around the turn of the fourteenth century. The Hall has been the scene of some of the most momentous events and ceremonies in English history, including the trials of Guy Fawkes and Charles I. Weighing 600 tons, the lofty hammerbeam-roof is supported by massive external buttresses and is the earliest example of its kind in England. Stone figures of English Kings line the south wall under the protective gaze of carved wooden angels bearing shields.

LANCASTER HOUSE, ST JAMES'S

*B*EGUN in 1825 for Frederick, Duke of York, younger brother of George IV, Lancaster House was completed in 1838 by the Duke of Sutherland, whose descendants sold it in 1912 to soap millionaire Sir William Lever. Lever did the patriotic thing and presented the house to the nation as a suitably impressive setting for state functions. Many of the interiors date from the 1820s and are decorated in the 'Louis Quatorze' or 'Versailles' style. The Staircase Hall (*above*) is later, an interior of the 1830s, equally opulent, but Italian in inspiration rather than French.

HOUSE OF LORDS, WESTMINSTER

*T*HE construction of the House of Lords began in 1840 and involved some of the greatest artists and craftsmen of the day. The walls of the Princes' Chamber (*right*) are decorated with bronze reliefs by William Theed representing important events from Tudor history and with portraits by Frederick Crace of Henry VIII and his wives.

FOREIGN OFFICE, WHITEHALL

*T*HE Durbar Court (*overleaf*) completed in 1866, originally formed part of the India Office, and was open to the sky, with bear pits let into the floor to give it a suitably sub-continental atmosphere. A glass roof has since been added and the floor covered over in marble.

THE FRENCH AMBASSADOR'S RESIDENCE, KENSINGTON

*B*UILT in 1840 for the Duke of Marlborough, No. 11 Kensington Palace Gardens was acquired by the French in 1944. The interiors are decorated throughout with seventeenth- and eighteenth-century French furniture and pictures, and the walls of the Private Dining Room *(above)* are clad with Louis XV panelling rushed to London from a château near Paris in preparation for a presidential visit shortly after the Second World War. France may be a republic, but the decoration of its London embassy is unashamedly *Ancien Régime*.

THE BRAZILIAN AMBASSADOR'S RESIDENCE, MAYFAIR

*S*INCE 1940 Plymouth House in Mount Street has been the official residence of the Brazilian Ambassador to Britain. The house dates from the late 1890s and takes its name from the man who built it, Lord Plymouth, a wealthy industrialist and collector. Much of the marble used in the decoration of the dramatic Entrance Hall and first-floor Lobby *(above)* came from Plymouth's own quarries at Penarth. It is quite the most spectacular embassy in London.

LIVERY HALLS

APOTHECARIES' HALL, BLACKFRIARS

*T*HE Apothecaries' Company was founded in 1617 and is still involved in the education and examination of pharmacists. The Hall *(above)* was built a few years after the Great Fire, on the site of an earlier building, and much of the woodwork is original. A minstrels' gallery at the north end is surmounted by the royal coat of arms, while a portrait of Gideon Delaune, apothecary to Queen Anne, hangs in a prominent position below, accompanied by a chest donated by one of the company's founding members, William Clarke.

STATIONERS' & NEWSPAPERMAKERS' COMPANY, AVE MARIA LANE

*F*ROM 1557 to 1710 all books legally published in England had to be registered with the Stationers' Guild, which also had the honour of burning heretical books. In 1933 the Stationers merged with the Newspapermakers, and today the team devotes its energies to charitable work. The Hall *(right)* dates from 1673 and retains its original carved screen. Armorial and military flags hang from projecting shafts in the wall, and figures associated with literature and printing, appear in the stained glass windows, which were added in 1888.

DRAPERS' COMPANY, THROGMORTON STREET

*T*HE Drapers' Hall *(left)* may not be the oldest livery hall in London – it was built in 1902–10 – but it is certainly the grandest, and the Company has every reason to be proud of its recent restoration. The ceiling is painted with scenes from Shakespeare (the central panel depicts a scene from *The Tempest*), but the overall effect is that of a Roman arena.

ARMOURERS' AND BRAZIERS' HALL, MOORGATE

*P*IKES, shields, and coats of armour are proudly displayed on the walls of the Armourers' and Braziers' Hall, laid out here for an official banquet.

The building dates from 1840, but the history of the company can be traced back to the early fourteenth century. The Armourers and Braziers at one time controlled the trade in brass and copper articles, as well as edged tools, guns and armour. Their connection with metal is maintained today through the funding of research in metallurgy.

THE FISHMONGERS'
COMPANY,
LONDON BRIDGE

*T*HE Fishmongers' Company has
been in existence for over seven
hundred years with a hall near
London Bridge since 1434. The
present hall was completed in 1834
and is a fine example of Greek
Revival architecture and
decoration. Despite extensive bomb
damage during the Second World
War and subsequent restoration,
the Drawing Room is particularly
impressive. Much of the furniture is
original, including a giltwood
console table supported by
dolphins, which serves as a
reminder of the Company's
connections with fishing and the
sea. One would never guess that
this and other interiors at the
Fishmongers' Hall had virtually
been rebuilt after catastrophic
bomb damage in the Blitz.

ACKNOWLEDGMENTS

My thanks must go first of all to James Ivory and Ismail Merchant who, in letting me loose on London in search of period locations for *Maurice*, first gave me the idea for this book. To my partner Peter Aprahamian, I owe an enormous debt of gratitude for months of excellent work, sometimes under conditions more conducive to mental breakdown than to good photography. No one could have brought more enthusiasm to the project, or greater tact, than my assistant Christiane Sherwen, whose support and encouragement were invaluable.

I have had the benefit of expert advice from a number of specialists in the field of architectural history and interior decoration. For giving so generously of their unique experience and knowledge, I should like to thank: Colin Amery, Clive Aslet, Marcus Binney, Dorothy Bosomworth, Stephen Calloway, Dan Cruickshank, Colin Cunningham, Dudley Dodd, Antony Feldman, Michael Gillingham, Mark Girouard, Roderick Gradidge, Stephen Jones, Michael Pick, John Martin Robinson, David Mlinaric, Joseph Morduant Crook, Alan Powers, Anne Saunders, Alistair Service, Gavin Stamp, Peter Thornton, Clive Wainwright, David Watkin and Roger White.

My thanks must also go to all the many local historians and borough councillors to whom I wrote for suggestions and who supplied me with much useful information: Barry Arden, Peter Barber, D. J. Catford, Mr Ellis, R. J. Evans, Gwynydd Gosling, J. Harding, P. Harness, Carl Harrison, R. J. Huntley, A. V. Mascull, David McDonald, Lilian Noble, A. J. Robinson, D. A. Ruddom, Joan Schwitzer, Richard A. Shaw, J. P. Tyrrell, Jane Vernan and E. J, West.

It is a duty, but above all a pleasure, to thank all those who kindly allowed photography and who submitted with such good grace to the chaos of flashlights, umbrellas, and yards of electric cable. My only regret is that I have not been able to include every interior we photographed. Carol Adams, Tony Adams, Mohamed Al Fayed, Simon Allen, Ian Angus, Pat Astley-Cooper, Sheila Ayres, Michael Bampton, His Excellency Vicomte Luc de la Barre de Nanteuil, G. Bates, Leslie Beaton, Meryl Beaumont, Graham Beck, Robin Bellwood, A. J. Bentley, Michael Bentley and Ronald Jones, Simon Berry, Elizabeth Bowes, Geraldine Bristow, Daria Brown, Michael T Brown, Robert Brown, Caroline Chubb, Stanley Comras, Sir Terence Conran, Chris Cooper, Colin Cooper, Sue Coppins, R. D. Corley, Julian Courtney, Ronald Cowe, Nicholas Crawley, Sue Cross, F. R. Dagnell, Julia Daniels, Paddy Drummond, Mike Dugdale, Michael Eagleton, Mrs Edwards, Mr and Mrs Ferguson, John Field, Peter Fyson, R. A. M. Forrest, Richard Garratt, Gordon Garretty, Myles Glover, John Graham-Leigh, Mr Gwynn, His Excellency Joao Hall Thermido, Peter Hames, Analisa Hamilton, John Harvey, R. Harvey, Paul Herbert, Henry Hoare, Felix Hope-Nicolson, Jean Hudson, Paula Hunt, J. E. Hok, Charles Jencks, Michele Julian, Mrs Killick, Mr Kimpton, Andrew Knight, H. E. Leif Leifland and Mrs Leifland, Mr M. T. N. Liddiard, Fiona Lindsay, W. Lindsay, David McKinstry, Jane McMorrow, P. Magnavacca, Julian Malone-Lee, Mr Martyn, Christine Mathez, John Mayhew, Christopher Mitchell, John Moran, Jim Morgan, Moira Mullen, Major Munthe, T. W. Nevin, Sister Nora, M. O'Brien, Major Charles O'Leary, John Oliver, D. G. Parry, Richard Parsons, Flight Ltnt Commander Paul Raine, Bill Roberts, Michael A. Roberts, Viscount Rothermere, Jacqueline Seabrook, Denis Seavers, Malcolm Smith, Richard Smith, W. C. Smith, Jeremy de Souza, Derek Stevens, William Stevenson, David Stileman, R. C. G. Strick, Peter Thornton, Annie Traherne, Patrick Trevor-Roper, R. J. Vardy, K. G. Varley, Claire Walsh, Giles Waterfield, Mark Webb, Sandra Weston, David Whisker, Stella Whitborn, Diane Williams, Mr Williams, A. W. Wilson and Mr Wyles.

The book's designer, James Campus, deserves a medal not only for his inspired work on the layout but also for physical endurance, having survived an inner-city ambush in which a good many of the photographs in this book were snatched at knife-point. Thanks are also due to Roger Sears, Editorial Director at Phaidon Press, who first saw the book's potential and who set the wheels in motion; to my editor Deirdre Headon, who kept me in line but never scolded; to my agent Xandra Hardie, whose patience and kindness are boundless; to Mark Fletcher and Sebastian Wormell, who helped compile the gazetteer; to Dolores Karney and Maria Seed, who did such an expert job of typing the manuscript; to all the many friends who accompanied me on long excursions in search of likely locations, especially Katya and Natasha Grenfell (fond memories of 'Maurice' days), Edward Harcourt, Stephen Hermer (who dreamed up the title), Emma-Louise O'Reilly, and David and Nassimah Reynolds; to my mother who took such an interest; and finally to Bridget, who carried me, kicking and screaming, over the final hurdle.

SELECT BIBLIOGRAPHY

HOWARD COLVIN, *A Biographical Dictionary of British Architects 1600–1840*, London, 1978.

MARK GIROUARD, *Victorian Pubs*, London, 1975.

ANTHONY LEJEUNE, *The Gentlemen's Clubs of London*, London, 1979.

IAN NAIRN, *Nairn's London*, London, 1966.

JOHN JULIUS NORWICH, *The Architecture of Southern England*, London, 1985.

SIR NIKOLAS PEVSNER & BRIDGET CHERRY, *Buildings of England Vols I & II*, London, reprinted 1985.

ANNE SAUNDERS, *The Art & Architecture of London*, Oxford, 1984.

ALASTAIR SERVICE, *The Architects of London from 1066 to the Present Day*, London, 1979.

Survey of London.

MALCOM WEBB, *Greater London's Suburban Cinemas*, Birmingham 1986.

GAZETTEER

....

SHOPS

R. ALLEN & CO. (BUTCHERS) LTD

Address: 117 Mount Street, W1H 6HX
Telephone: 0171 499 5831
Underground: Marble Arch or Green Park
Open for business: 4am–4pm Mon–Fri, 4am–12.30pm Sat.

Built 1886–7 to designs of James Trant-Smith; red brick facade with Queen Anne and Franco-Flemish motifs in terracotta; tiled interior virtually unchanged; famous for traditional shop displays.

AUSTIN REED

Address: 103–113 Regent Street, W1A 2AJ
Telephone: 0171 734 6789
Underground: Piccadilly Circus
Open for business: 9.30am–6pm Mon–Tues & Sat, 10am–6pm Wed, 9.30am–7pm Thurs–Fri, 11am–5pm Sun.

Edwardian Baroque exterior designed by Reginald Blomfield; Art Deco Barber shop in basement completed 1929–30 to designs of P.J. Westwood. Barber's beautifully restored and maintained: vitrolite panelling, Travertine marble floor, original barber's chairs by Osborne Garrett & Co.

BATES

Address: 21a Jermyn Street, SW1Y 6HP
Telephone: 0171 734 2722
Underground: Piccadilly Circus

Open for business: 9am–5.30pm Mon–Fri, 9.30am–4pm Sat.

Typical late Victorian hatter; located on ground floor of Gordon Chambers, residential/commercial development completed 1897 to designs of Edward Keynes Porchase, architect of Mallett in Bond Street [q.v.].

BERRY BROS.

Address: 3 St James's Street, SW1A 1EG
Telephone: 0171 396 9666
Underground: Green Park
Open for business: 9am–5.30pm Mon–Fri, 10am–4pm Sat.

Wine merchants; established late seventeenth century; still in family ownership; site of shop originally occupied by farm house converted 1676 as coffee shop; site redeveloped 1731–5 to create present premises; ground floor interior largely unchanged; wooden floor, panelled walls, weighing beams, shelves lined with old bottles, Victorian furniture; Arts and Crafts Dining Room on first floor with de Morgan tiles.

HARRODS

Address: Brompton Road, SW1X 7XL
Telephone: 0171 730 1234
Underground: Knightsbridge
Open for business: 10am–6pm Mon–Tues & Sat, 10am–7pm Wed–Fri.

One of the earliest and best preserved department stores in London; business founded by Henry Charles Harrod 1835; began as grocery; originally situated in Stepney; moved to Brompton Road, Knightsbridge, 1849; gradual expansion to fill present island site 1911; main block erected 1901–03 to designs of Charles W. Stephens, architect of Claridges's [q.v.]; Basil Street facade added by Louis D. Blanc 1929–30; many surviving details within; ornate Edwardian plasterwork in principal interiors along Brompton Road; virtuoso tile work in meat Hall, execute 1901–03 by Doulton's to designs of W.J. Neatby; Edwardian showcases in Jewellery Department; Classical Revival Luggage Department dating from late 1920s; suite of 1930s interiors in basement below Man's Shop: Jacobean Revival Saloon, Moderne Gentlemen's Lavatory and Art Deco Barber Shop.

MALLETT & SON (ANTIQUES) LTD

Address: 40 New Bond Street, W! 0BS
Telephone: 0171 499 7411
Underground: Bond Street
Open for business: 9.15am–5.45pm Mon–Fri, 11am–4pm Sat.

Baroque Revival exterior designed *c.*1905 by E. Keynes Porchase, architect of Bates [q.v.]; acquired by Mallett; interior with Italianate grotto designed by Raymond Erith 1968.

MALLETT AT BOURDON BOUSE LTD

Address: Bourdon House, Davies Street, W1Y 1LJ
Telephone: 0171 929 2444
Underground: Bond Street

Open for business: 9.30am–5.30pm Mon–Fri.

Early Georgian town house built 1721–5; extended in mid-eighteenth century and again in 1909–10; occupied by Duke of Westminster 1917–53; acquired by Mallet after Duchess of Westminster's death, 1957; interior well preserved; Georgian staircase with carved treads and turned balusters; much original woodwork; shellwork grotto on first floor by Gordon Davies, 1975; furnished throughout with finest antiques.

W. MARTYN'S

Address: 135 Muswell Hill Broadway, N10 3RS
Telephone: 0181 883 5642
Underground: Finsbury Park, then W7 bus to Muswell Hill Broadway
Open for business: 9.30am–5.30pm Mon–Wed & Fri, 9.30am–1pm Thurs, 9am–5.30pm Sat.

Established 1897 as general grocery; now specializing in tea, coffee and fine foods; known locally as 'the Fortnum & Mason of Muswell Hill'; still in

family ownership after four generations; interior virtually unchanged; wooden floor and counters, barley twist shelving, late Victorian merchandising.

JAMES SMITH

Address: 53 New Oxford Street, WC1A 1BL
Telephone: 0171 836 4731
Underground: Tottenham Court Road
Open for business: 9.30am–5.20pm

Mon–Fri, 10am–5pm Sat.

Umbrella makers; business founded 1830; moved to present premises (former dairy) 1856; shopfront emblazoned with painted signs; interior virtually unchanged since Victorian times. *(Pictured previous column)*

TESSIERS

Address: 26 New Bond Street, W1Y 0JY
Telephone: 0171 629 0458
Underground: Bond Street
Open for business: 10am–5pm Mon–Fri,

10.30am–5pm Sat.

Jewellers and silversmiths; business established in late eighteenth century by Lewis Tessier, grandson of Huguenot exile said to be descended from Kings of Sicily; present shop opened by Tessier's sons, 1852; patronized by Queen Victoria and other members of the royal family; two changes of ownership before business acquired by great uncle of present owners, 1910; shop front and interior more or less unchanged since 1852; mahogany and looking-glass display cases set off by antique jewellery and silver; Corinthian columns framing door to rear; framed locks of hair providing reminder that Tessiers were originally 'artists in hair'.

....

RESTAURANTS

CAFE ROYAL

Address: 68 Regent Street, W1R 6EL
Telephone: 0171 437 9090
Underground: Piccadilly Circus
Open for business: 12 noon–2.30pm, 6pm–11pm daily.

Grill room completed 1865–72 to designs of Archer and Green, architects of Hyde Park Hotel; more or less unchanged despite reconstruction of building 1923–8 by Sir Henry Tanner, architect of Park Lane Hotel [q.v.]; jewel box effect, caryatids, resplendent mirrors, painted ceiling.

[FORMERLY] F. COOKE

Address: 41 Kingsland High Street, E8 2JL
Telephone: 0171 254 9322
Railway Station: Dalston Junction

Open for business: 10am–8pm Mon–Sat.

Until recently a traditional eel and pie shop, although still functioning as a cafe; business originally founded in Hackney 1862; restaurant illustrated opened 1910; palatial interior, tiled and mirrored with many original furnishings; one of the sights of London.

THE CRITERION

Address: 222 Piccadilly, W1 9LB
Telephone: 0171 930 0488
Underground: Piccadilly Circus
Open for business: 12 noon–2.30pm, 6pm–12midnight Mon–Sat, 12 noon–4pm, 6pm–10.30pm Sun.

Part of Criterion Theatre complex, built to designs of Thomas Verity 1870–4; present decoration thought to date from *c.*1905; gilt mosaic ceiling, Moorish arcades, marble carvings, some original light fittings; quite breathtaking.

RISTORANTE ITALIANO

Address: 54–5 Curzon Street, W1Y 7PF
Telephone: 0171 629 2742
Underground: Green Park
Open for business: 11.30am–3pm, 5.30–11.30pm Mon–Fri, 6–11.30pm Sat.

Rococo Revival interiors of *c.*1900 located on first floor of eighteenth-century town house; fibrous plaster C-scrolls, musical trophies etc; ideal setting for tête-à-têtes and private parties.

RULE'S

Address: 35 Maiden Lane, WC2
Telephone: 0171 836 5314
Underground: Covent Garden
Open for business: 12 noon–12 midnight Mon–Sat.

Restaurant founded 1798; interior of present building completed *c.*1890; frequented by King Edward VII and his mistress Lily Langtry; public and private dining rooms with immense charm and period atmosphere; many original furnishings.

SAGNE MAISON PATISSERIE (PATISSERIE VALERIE)

Address: 105 Marylebone High Street, W1M 3DB
Telephone: 0171 935 6240
Underground: Baker Street
Open for business: 8am–7pm Mon–Sat, 9am–6pm Sun.

Founded 1921 by Swiss pastry-lover M. Sagne. Interior retains strong Continental atmosphere; inlaid woodwork and murals representing landscapes with classical ruins.

SIMPSON'S-IN-THE-STRAND

Address: 100 Strand, WC2R 0EW
Telephone: 0171 836 9112
Underground: Charing Cross
Open for business: 12 noon–2.30pm, 6pm–11pm Mon–Sat, 12 noon–2pm, 6–9pm Sun.

Founded 1828; remodelled and decorated 1890s by Thomas Colcutt, architect of Lloyds Register of Shipping [q.v.]; Adam Revival interiors on first floor; Arts and Crafts Dining Room on ground floor; many original furnishings; traditional English fare.

....

HOTELS

CLARIDGE'S

Address: Brook Street, W1A 2JQ
Telephone: 0171 629 8860
Underground: Bond Street

Hotel founded 1854 by William and Marianne Claridge, succeeded by Claridge's Hotel Company 1881; acquired 1892 by Richard D'Oyly Carte, theatrical impresario and owner of Savoy Hotel in the Strand; original building pulled down and replaced 1895–9; shell designed by C.W. Stephens, architect of the Brompton Road facade of Harrods [q.v.]; decoration of interior entrusted to Sir Ernest George; 1929–36 alterations and additions by Oswald Milne;

spectacular public rooms and private suites beautifully maintained by management and staff; surviving decoration and furniture from 1890s through to late 1930s.

THE DORCHESTER

Address: Park Lane, W1A 2HJ
Telephone: 0171 629 8888
Underground: Hyde Park Corner

Begun to designs of Owen Jones but completed 1930 by William Curtis Green, architect of Barclays Bank, Piccadilly [q.v.]; new wing added 1953 with penthouse suite by stage designer Oliver Messel; Messel rooms little changed; rest of hotel extensively modernized. *(Pictured previous column)*

GREAT EASTERN HOTEL

Address: Liverpool Street, EC2M 2QN
Telephone: 0171 928 5151 for further information
Underground: Liverpool Street

Hotel closed for major refurbishment. Admission to Freemasons' Temple restricted; any applications should be made in writing. Main block completed to designs of Charles Barry; Freemasons' Temple added 1912 by Brown and Barrow.

INVERNESS COURT HOTEL

Address: Inverness Terrace, W2 3JL
Telephone: 0171 229 1444
Underground: Bayswater or Queensway

Built around the turn of the century by prominent Victorian businessman for mistress; extraordinary range of bizarre interiors including Viennese-style private theatre (now used as a bar), Louis XVI-style Salon, Victorian Drawing Room, early Georgian Conference Room and Baroque Staircase.

PARK LANE HOTEL

Address: Piccadilly, W1
Telephone: 0171 499 6321
Underground: Green Park

Built *c.*1927 for Yorkshire magnate

St Pancras Hotel

Sir Bracewell Smith to designs by Henry Tanner; surviving 1920s decoration in Foyer and Ball Room; some original furniture.

St Pancras Hotel

Address: Euston Road, NW1 2QL
Telephone: 0171 304 3900
Underground: King's Cross/St Pancras
Contact London Continental Railways on above number for information about guided tours.

Built 1873–8 to designs by Sir George Gilbert Scott for London Midland and Scottish Railway Company; originally known as Midland

Grand Hotel; closed down and converted into offices 1935; hybrid of English and Continental Gothic; superb ironwork and stencilled decoration in Staircase Compartment; many other fine interiors; awaiting restoration.

The Savoy

Address: Strand, WC2R 0EU
Telephone: 0171 836 4343
Underground: Charing Cross
Stands on site of medieval Palace of Savoy; built in two stages: first block along river completed 1889, second block facing Strand erected 1903–04; exteriors designed by Thomas Collcutt, architect of Lloyd's Register of Shipping and Simpsons-in-the-Strand [q.v.]; decoration of interiors entrusted to Arts and Crafts designer Arthur H. Mackmurdo; river front suites later redecorated in Louis XV/Louis XVI style by paris *décorateur* René Sergent; metallic Art Deco fascia added to Strand front by Murray Easton and Howard Robertson 1929; public rooms extensively redecorated 1926–9 by Basil Ionides, who also worked on interiors of adjoining Savoy Theatre and Claridge's [q.v.]; many surviving details, including allegorical frieze and foliated handrails in Foyer (1880s), *dixhuitième* panelling and overdoors in bedrooms

overlooking river (*c.*1905), naval columns and tassel panelling in Pinafore Room (1920s), and etched looking-glass recess on approach to Ball Room (1920s); some period furniture.

....

CLUBS & SOCIETIES

Gentlemen's Clubs are not generally open to visitors other than members and their guests but it is worth applying in writing to the Secretary.

Athenaeum Club

Address: Pall Mall, SW1Y 5ER
Telephone: 0171 930 4843
Underground: Piccadilly Circus
(Shown above) Founded as a club for

artists and men of letters 1824; designed by Decimus Burton and completed 1827–30; attic storey added 1899–1900 by Thomas Collcutt, architect of Simpson's-in-the-Strand [q.v.]; several splendid interiors, notably Entrance Hall, Coffee Room (restored), Smoking Room and Library; many original features.

Brooks's

Address: St James's Street, SW1A 1LN
Telephone: 0171 493 4411
Underground: Green Park
(Shown above) Founded 1764; clubhouse built 1776–8 to designs by Henry Holland; rear annexe by John MacVicar Anderson 1889; surviving eighteenth-century decoration, including painted panels, plasterwork, chimney pieces, pier glasses and overmantels; Great Subscription Room (immaculately restored after fire), Library and Staircase Hall are of special interest;

fine collection of portraits and antique furniture.

The Reform Club

Address: Pall Mall, SW1Y 5EW
Telephone: 0171 930 9374
Underground: Piccadilly Circus
Club founded 1836 for champions of electoral reform; clubhouse erected 1838–41 to designs of Sir Charles Barry, architect of House of Lords and Travellers' Club [q.v.]; exterior based on Palazzo Farnese in Rome; interiors of similar extraction: Great Hall, Library, Morning Room and Staircase are very fine; many original furnishings.

The Royal Automobile Club

Address: 89 Pall Mall, SW1Y 5HS
Telephone: 0171 930 2345
Underground: Piccadilly Circus or Green Park
Club founded 1897 for 'Protection, Encouragement and Development of Automobilism'; clubhouse designed by Anglo-French partnership of Arthur davis and Charles Mèwes, architects of Ritz Hotel; built 1908–11 on site of old War Office; Place de la Concorde exterior and many splendid interiors, including Louis XVI-style Dining Room and Byzantine Swimming Pool.

The Royal society

Address: 6 Carlton House Terrace, SW1Y 5AG
Telephone: 0171 839 5561
Underground: Piccadilly Circus
Originally built as palatial town house by John Nash *c.*1830; interior redecorated 1889–90 for Buenos Aires millionaire C.H. Sanford by Sir Ernest George; home of Royal Society since 1967; replica of Quattrocento Florentine Palazzo; spectacular marble Entrance Hall and Staircase, exquisite carvings, inlaid doors, mother-of-pearl ceiling and allegorical paintings.

The Travellers' Club

Address: 106 Pall Mall, SW1 5EP
Telephone: 0171 930 8688
Underground: Piccadilly Circus
Club founded 1819 'to form a point of reunion for gentlemen who have travelled abroad and to afford them the opportunity of inviting as honorary visitors the principal members of all foreign missions and travellers of distinction'; clubhouse built 1829–32 by Sir Charles Barry, architect of Reform Club and House of Lords [q.v.]; pioneering exercise in Palazzo style; many grand interiors, of which library is most impressive; fine collection of pictures and furniture.

....

PUBLIC HOUSES

The Blackfriar

Address: 174 Queen Victoria Street, EC4V 4BY
Telephone: 0171 236 5650
Underground: Blackfriars
Open for business: 11.30am–10pm Mon–Fri. *(Shown above)*
Uniquely fine example of Arts and Crafts pub, built 1905 to designs of architect H. Fuller Clark and sculptor Henry Poole; streetfront and interior well preserved; jolly barrel-vaulted chamber to rear, decorated with marble, mosiacs and bronze reliefs and figures on mock-monastic theme.

The Red Lion

Address: 2 Duke of York Street, St James's SW1 6JY
Telephone: 0171 930 2030
Underground: Piccadilly Circus
Open for business: 11am–11pm Mon–Sat.
Established in or before 1788; original pub rebuilt 1821; present interior designed by W.H. Rawlings 1871; much original decoration; lincrusta ceiling, mahogany woodwork and spectacular virtuoso glasswork attributed to Walter Gibbs & Sons of Southwark.

The Salisbury

Address: 1 Grand Parade, Haringey, N4
Telephone: 0181 800 3600
Underground: Manor House
Open for business: 11am–11pm Mon–Sat, 12 noon–10.30pm Sun.
Grandiose late Victorian gin palace by north London builder John Cathles Hill; opened 1899; terrazzo floors, stained and etched glass, painted tiles, wrought-ironwork; quite overpowering.

YE OLDE CHESHIRE CHEESE

Address: 145 Fleet Street, EC4E 4BU
Telephone: 0171 353 6170
Underground: Blackfriars
Open for business, Bar: 11.30am–11pm
Mon–Sat; Restaurant: 12 noon–3pm,
6–9pm Mon–Fri, 12 noon–3pm,
6–8.30pm Sat, 12 noon–3pm Sun.

Traditional pub and chop house;
erected 1677; street front altered *c.*1820;
reputedly frequented by Dr Johnson,
who occupied nearby house in Gough
Square [q.v.]; atmospheric interior.

....

DOMESTIC INTERIORS

CHARLTON HOUSE

Address: Charlton House Community
Centre, Charlton Road, Charlton SE7
8RE
Telephone: 0181 856 3951
Railway Station: Charlton
Admission: by prior arrangement

Jacobean manor house built
1607–12 for Sir Adam Newton, tutor
to Henry, Prince of Wales, eldest son
of James I; attributed to John Thorpe;
minor alterations 1659; restored and
enlarged by Norman Shaw 1877–8;
privately owned until 1925 when
acquired by local authority; unusual
two-storey Hall; original plasterwork
and chimney pieces in Saloon, Long
Gallery and White Drawing Room.

NO. 18 FOLGATE STREET

Address: 18 Folgate Street, Spitalfields,
E1 6BX
Underground: Liverpool Street

Terraced house erected 1724;
acquired and transformed by American
Dennis Severs; ingenious antiquarian
interiors in every style of decoration
from early eighteenth to late nineteenth
century.

HAM HOUSE

Address: Richmond, Surrey, TW10 7RS
Telephone: 0181 940 1950
Underground: Richmond, then bus 371 to
Royal Oak, Ham.
Open: end March–end October, 1–5pm
daily except Thurs/Fri.

Built 1610 for Sir Thomas
Vavasour, Earl Marshal to James I;
extensive alterations 1637–9 for William
Murray, 1st Earl of Dysart; enlarged
and aggrandized 1670s for Dysart's
daughter after marriage to Duke of
Lauderdale; new furniture added 1727
by 4th Earl of Dysart, who ordered
insertion of sash windows; remained in
family ownership until 1948 when

presented to National Trust; restored to
a rare degree of accuracy; many fine
interiors with original furnishings.

LEIGHTON HOUSE

Address: 12 Holland Park Road, W14
8L7
Telephone: 0171 602 3316
Underground: High Street Kensington
Open: 11am–5.30pm Mon–Sat except
Bank Holidays.

Begun 1865 as studio and town
house for Frederick, Lord Leighton,
President of the Royal Academy and
only English artist to be elevated to the
peerage; designed by Leighton in
partnership with architect George
Aitchison; studio extended 1869–70;
Arab Hall added 1877–9; converted

into museum after Leighton's death;
subsequently acquired by local council;
several fascinating interiors beautifully
restored and cared for by curator;
important collection of Victorian
paintings.

LINLEY SAMBOURNE HOUSE

Address: 16 Stafford Terrace, W8 7BH
Telephone: 0181 742 3438 (Victorian
Society)
Underground: High Street Kensington
Open: 10am–4pm Wed, 2pm–5pm Sun,
Mar–Oct.

Victorian terraced house occupied
1874–1910 by Linley Sambourne, chief
political cartoonist at *Punch*, remained
in family ownership until 1980 when
presented to Victorian Society and
opened to public; perfectly-preserved
example of 'Artistic' style in interior
decoration; full complement of original
furnishings.

LITTLE HOLLAND HOUSE

Address: 40 Beeches Avenue,
Carshalton, Surrey, SN5 3LW
Telephone: 0181 253 1009 (Croydon and

Carshalton Tourist Office) for further
details.
Railway Station: Carshalton Beeches
Open: 12 noon–6pm first Sun of each
month Mar–Oct and Sun and Mon of
easter, Spring and Summer Bank
Holidays.

Arts and Crafts house built 1902–04
by original occupant, Frank Dickinson,
self-taught artist/craftsman and
visionary disciple of William Morris;
acquired from Dickinson's heirs by
local authority 1972; virtually
unchanged since Dickinson's death;
wealth of furniture and artefacts
designed and hand-crafted by
Dickinson himself.

MARBLE HILL HOUSE

Address: Richmond Road, Twickenham,
Middlesex, TW1 2NL
Telephone: 0181 892 5115
Underground: Richmond
Open: 10am–6pm daily except
Mon/Tues Easter – end Oct,
10am–4pm otherwise.

Palladian villa built 1724–9 for
Henrietta Howard, Countess of Suffolk,
and a mistress of George II; original
plan by Colen Campbell; final
execution by Roger Morris with
assistance from Henry Herbert, later
9th Earl of Pembroke; Dining Room
altered 1750–1 by Matthew Brettingham;
privately-owned until 1902 when
acquired by LCC; restored as public
museum by GLC 1965–6; house small
but stately, befitting rank of original
occupant; incompletely furnished but
architectural decoration intact.

THE OCTAGON, ORLEANS HOUSE

Address: Orleans House Gallery,
Riverside, Middlesex, TW1 3DJ
Telephone: 0181 892 0221
Underground: Richmond
Open: 1–5.30pm Tues–Sat (1–4.30pm
Oct–May), 2–5.30pm Sun (2.30–4.30pm
Oct–May), 2–5.30pm Easter, Spring
and Summer Bank Holidays.

Domed octagonal pavilion built
1720 to designs of James Gibbs with
virtuoso plasterwork by Giovanni
Bagutti and Giuseppe Artari; setting for
official reception of George II's new
Queen, Caroline Anspach, 1729;
originally situated in grounds of large

house built 1710 by John James for
James Johnston; house occupied
1815–17 by Louis Philippe Duc
d'Orléans, later King of France, hence
name; octagon saved from destruction
by Hon. Mrs Levy when house
demolished 1927; bequeathed to local
authority 1962.

OSTERLEY PARK HOUSE

Address: Isleworth, TW7 4RB
Telephone: 0181 560 3918
Underground: Osterley
Open: 2–5pm Wed–Sun, April 1–Oct
31; Park open year-round

House of 1578 remodelled for
banker Robert Child by Robert Adam
1763–80; privately owned until 1949
when presented to National Trust;
restored with great flair and sympathy;
many fine interiors with original
furnishings.

SIR JOHN SOANE MUSEUM

Address: 13 Lincoln's Inn Fields, WC2
3BP
Telephone: 0171 405 2107
Underground: Holborn
Open: 10am–5pm Tues–Sat; 6-9pm first
Tues each month; closed Bank
Holidays and Christmas Eve.

Early nineteenth-century town house
built, occupied and bequeathed to
nation by architect Sir John Soane;
virtually untouched since Soane's death;
not to be missed. *(Shown next column)*

SOUTHSIDE HOUSE

Address: Woodhayes Road, Wimbledon
Common, SW19 4RJ
Telephone: 0181 946 7643
Underground: Wimbledon
Open: guided tours Jan 1–June 24, 2, 3
and 4pm Tues, Thurs, Sat.

Seventeenth-century farm house
extensively rebuilt and aggrandized in
eighteenth century; still in family
ownership; beguiling antiquarian
interiors made up of fragments and
furnishings from different periods,
some original to house perhaps, but

most, one imagines, assembled nineteenth century; fascinating web of fact and fiction.

THEATRES AND CINEMAS

For access to auditoria it is best to apply in writing. Foyers are generally open to the street.

THE BRIXTON ACADEMY

Address: 211 Stockwell Road, SW9 9SL
Telephone: 0171 274 1525
Underground: Brixton
Admission: restricted to concerts.

Grand 'atmospheric' cinema completed 1929 to designs of Edward A. Stone; seating capacity 2,982; opening show 'The Singing Fool'; closed 1972 with 'Red Sun' and 'The Looking Glass War'; reopened as venue for live shows 1982; half-domed classical entrance hall; Art Deco foyer; outlandish auditorium with proscenium arch forming Italian Renaissance villa and garden complex, complete with statues, artificial vegetation and ceiling painted to represent star-lit sky.

THE LONDON COLISEUM

Address: St Martin's Lane, WC2N 4ES
Telephone: 0171 836 7700
Underground: Leicester Square or Charing Cross

Lavish music hall built 1903–04 for impressario Oswald Stoll by Frank Matcham, architect of Hackney Empire [q.v.]; occupied since August 1968 by English National Opera; Foyer sadly whitewashed; auditorium well preserved.

HACKNEY EMPIRE

Address: 291 Mare Street, E8 1EJ
Telephone: 0181 985 2424/0181 800 8233 (Friends of Hackney Empire)
Underground: Bethnal Green

Admission by prior arrangement with Friends of Hackney Empire.
Built for theatrical impressario Oswald Stoll by Frank Matcham, architect of London Coliseum [q.v.], Sadlers Wells and Richmond Theatre; opulent interior consciously modelled on grand opera houses of Italy; front of theatre decorated by J.M. Boekbinder; auditorium by De Jong; acquired by Mecca organization and converted into bingo hall, 1966; taken over by Hackney Empire Preservation Trust, 1986; undergoing programme of restoration and fund-raising.

NEW RAINBOW THEATRE

Address: Seven Sisters Road, Finsbury Park, N4 3NX
Underground: Finsbury Park

Originally Astoria, Finsbury Park; 'atmospheric' cinema completed 1930 to designs of Edward A. Stone, architect of Brixton Academy [q.v.]; acquired by Odeon chain 1970; closed as cinema 1971; converted into Dance Hall and venue for rock concerts; acquired by New Rainbow Trust 1987.

THE PLAYHOUSE THEATRE

Address: Northumberland Avenue, WC2N 4DE
Telephone: 0171 839 4401/0171 839 4292 (Stage Door)
Underground: Charing Cross
Admission by prior arrangement with Stage Door.

Completed 1906 to designs of Detmar Blow and Fernand Billerey; interior restored; drop curtain and painted panels on walls and ceiling of auditorium by Henri Brémond and Maurice Tastemain; allegorical figures over proscenium arch and caryatids supporting boxes by Louis Noël and Déchin.

THEATRE ROYAL DRURY LANE

Address: Catherine Street, WC2B 5JF
Telephone: 0171 836 3352
Underground: Covent Garden
Admission by written application.

Built 1811–12 to designs of Benjamin Wyatt; fourth theatre to be erected on site (first erected 1663); interior remodelled 1831 by Samuel Beazley, architect and playwright; auditorium remodelled 1901 by Philip Pilditch and again 1921–2 by J. Emblin-walker, assisted by Edward Jones and Robert Crombie; Greek Doric vestibule; domed Foyer; Empire Style auditorium; large collection of paintings and statues on theatrical theme; parts of building sadly spoilt by refurbishment. *(Pictured next column)*

SAVOY THEATRE

Address: Strand, WC2
Telephone: 0171 836 8888
Underground: Charing Cross
Admission to auditorium by written application.

Built 1884 by C.J. Phipps for Richard D'Oyly Carte, owner of adjoining hotel; interior completely redecorated 1929 by Basil Ionides, who also worked at Savoy Hotel and Claridges [q.v.], assisted by Gilbert Seale; finest and best preserved theatre of its date in London.

TOOTING GRANADA

Address: 58 Mitcham Road, SW17 9NA
Telephone: 0181 672 5717
Underground: Tooting Broadway
Admission by written application to Gala Tooting.

Originally cinema, now Bingo Club; completed 1931; exterior by Cecil Masey and R.H. Uren; interior by Theodore Komisarjevsky; vast auditorium seating more than 3,000; opening show 'Oh! Oh! Cleopatra!'; closed as cinema 1973 with 'The Good, the Bad and The Ugly'; medieval-style Foyer; Alhambra Hall of Mirrors; auditorium conceived as Gothic cathedral; many original furnishings, including gold-painted Gothic bench on half-landing of main Staircase.

OFFICES

Offices are not generally open to the public, except on business, but tours can sometimes be arranged and it is worth applying in writing for details.

LICHFIELD HOUSE (CLERICAL MEDICAL INVESTMENT GROUP LTD)

Address: 15 St James's Square, SW1Y 4LQ
Telephone: 0171 930 5474 (extension 3431)
Underground: Green Park
Admission by prior application.

Neo-classical town house built

1764–6 for Thomas Anson by James 'Athenian' Stuart; first terraced house in London with Greek Temple facade; alterations 1791–4 for Anson's sons by Samuel Wyatt; acquired 1856 by Clerical Medical Life Assurance Society and converted for use as office block; ground floor extensively remodelled 1928; several interiors with surviving decoration by Stuart and Wyatt, most complete being Board Room and Committee Room. *(Pictured below)*

CROMWELL HOUSE

Address: The Bank, 104 Highgate Hill, N6
Underground: Archway

Family house built *c.*1640; extensively restored after fire, 1866; virtuoso brick exterior; Staircase Compartment with surviving seventeenth-century woodwork.

FORMER DAILY EXPRESS BUILDING

Address: Fleet Street, EC4
Underground: Blackfriars

Futuristic office block built 1931–2 by Ellis, Clarke and Atkinson in partnership with Sir Owen Williams; outlandish Art Deco Entrance Hall designed by Robert Atkinson with metal-work reliefs representing colonial enterprise, chromium handrails forming twisted serpents and ribbed ceiling with pendentive bosses recalling interior of medieval chapter house. Now split-up into retail premises.

FORMER DAILY MAIL BUILDING

Address: Carmelite House, Carmelite Street, EC4
Underground: Blackfriars

Completed 1899 to designs of Herbert Ellis and William Clarke; Art Nouveau murals and elaborate ironwork lift shaft and balustrade in Staircase Hall; Napoloenic Board Room with pedimented mahogany bookcases surmounted by classical murals c.1905.

KENT HOUSE (EAGLE STAR)

Address: 22 Arlington Street
Telephone: 0171 493 8411
Underground: Green Park
Admission by written application.
Palladian town house completed 1755 to designs of William Kent for then Prime Minister, Henry Pelham; building remodelled 1840–52 by Owen Jones and refaced 1854–6 by William Burn for 11th Duke of Hamilton; purchased 1870 by millionaire industrialist Ivor Bertie Guest, later Lord Wimbourne, and extensively altered and enlarged; turned over 1939 to Red Cross; acquired 1946 by Eagle Star Insurance Company; restored in recent years; sumptuous range of period interiors dating from mid-eighteenth to early twentieth century.

SPENCER HOUSE

Address: 27 St James's Place, SW1A 1NR
Telephone: 0171 499 8620
Underground: Green Park
Open: 11.45am–4.45pm Sun; closed Jan and Aug.
Early Neoclassical town house built 1755–65 for John, 1st Earl Spencer; shell erected and ground floor decorated 1755–8 by John Vardy, pupil of William Kent, under supervision of General George Gray, amateur architect and Secretary of Society of Dilettanti; first floor decorated and in part remodelled 1758–66 by James 'Athenian' Stuart, architect of Lichfield House [q.v.]; ground floor redecorated and in part remodelled for 2nd Earl Spencer 1785–92 by Henry Holland, architect of Brooks's Club [q.v.]; first floor restored and ground floor redecorated by Parisian *tapissier* 1871; handed over to National Nursing Agency in Second World war; doors, chimney pieces, chair rails and other fixtures removed to Althorp for safe-keeping during Blitz and subsequently incorporated into state apartments there; house let since War to Christie's, British Oxygen Company, *The Economist* magazine and J. Rothschild Holdings; original plasterwork and some woodwork in principal apartments on ground and first floors; painted panels and murals in Painted Room; recently fully restored to former grandeur at a cost of £1.6m.

LLOYDS REGISTER OF SHIPPING

Address: 71 Fenchurch Street, EC3M 4BS
Telephone: 0171 709 9166
Underground: Monument
Closed for refurbishment; due to reopen 1999.
Built 1900–01 to designs of Thomas Collcutt, architect of Simpson's-in-the-Strand [q.v.]; extraordinary cross between Edwardian Baroque and Arts and Crafts; principal interior with murals and ceiling paintings by Frank Brangwyn, gerald Moira and E.J. Lambert; surviving decoration also in Library and Staircase Hall.

OAK ROOM (THAMES WATER)

Address: New River Head, Rosebery Avenue, EC1R 4TO
Underground: Angel
Admission by written application.
Late seventeenth-century panelled interior located in 1920s office block; superb carving by Grinling Gibbons, exuberant Baroque plasterwork and allegorical portrait of William III on ceiling by court painter Henry Cooke; originally part of Cistern House (name later changed to Water House), built 1613 on same site as headquarters of New River Company, privately-owned business which, with technical assistance of engineer Hugh Myddleton and financial backing of James I, brought fresh water to London via twenty-five mile channel from Hertfordshire to supplement diminishing local supplies; new River Company taken over 1902 by Metropolitan Water Board which purchased Oak Room 1904 for £2,000; Water House torn down 1920 and replaced by present building designed by Austen Hall; Oak Room saved from destruction and incorporated into new structure; slightly altered in process; dismantled and stored during Blitz; reinstated 1945; Metropolitan Water Board absorbed by Thames Water 1973.

NO. 8 CLIFFORD STREET

Address: 8 Clifford Street, W1X 1RB
Underground: Green Park
Admission by written application.
Grand town house built 1719; occupied until 1748 by Thomas Walker MP, art-lover and high-ranking government official; remained in family ownership until 1830 when sold to Bethel Walrond who later married daughter of Earl of Rosslyn; in use as tailor's showroom and workshop 1850; divided up into rented units by 1900; acquired 1931 by J. Lyons & Co., and converted into a tea shop; subsequently used as an office building; remarkable for original painted Staircase Compartment attributed to Sir James Thornhill; later decorative painting on first floor.

....

BANKS

BANK OF ENGLAND

Address: Threadneedle Street, EC2R 8AH
Telephone: 0171 601 5545
Underground: Bank
Museum open 10am–5pm Mon–Fri.
Bank founded 1694; operated at first from Mercer's Hall, then from Grocer's Hall; present site acquired 1724; first building completed 1732 to designs of George Sampson; enlarged by Sir Robert Taylor 1764–6 and by Sir John Soane 1788–1808; extensively remodelled and enlarged by Sir Herbert Baker 1921–37; nationalized 1946; little surviving decoration besides Taylor Court Room, hoisted by Baker from ground to first floor and 'improved'. *(Shown next column)*

BARCLAYS BANK PICCADILLY BRANCH

Address: 160 Piccadilly, W1A 2AB
Telephone: 0171 445 3200
Underground: Green Park
Banking Hall Open: 9.30am–3.30pm Mon–Fri.
Built 1922 to designs of William Curtis Green, architect of Dorchester Hotel [q.v.]; originally car showroom for Wolseley Motors Ltd; acquired by barclays 1926 and converted for use as bank by original architect; exotic oriental-style interiors with matching furniture. *(Shown next column)*

C. HOARE & CO.

Address: 37 Fleet Street, EC4P 4DQ
Telephone: 0171 445 3200
Underground: Temple
Banking Hall Open: 9.30am–3.30pm

Family-owned bank founded in or before 1673; premises on present site since 1690; present building begun 1829 to designs of Charles Parker; alterations and additions 1929 by Herbert Baker; main block largely unchanged since early nineteenth century; restrained Italianate facade; Classical Banking Hall with stone floor, oak panelling, original oil-burning stove with Greek Revival frieze of gilded honeysuckle and porters in period costume; museum room on first floor.

LLOYDS LAW COURTS BRANCH

Address: 222 Strand, WC2R 1BB
Telephone: 0345 300004
Underground: Temple
Banking Hall Open: 9,30am–3.30pm Mon–Fri.
Originally a restaurant and club for lawyers; designed by W.Wimble and Goymour Cuthbert; completed 1883; acquired by Lloyds 1895; entrance decorated with Doulton tiles representing flowers and characters from history and literature; remains of similar decoration within.

HOSPITALS

GROVELANDS PRIORY HOSPITAL

Address: The Bourne, Southgate, N14 6RA
Underground: Southgate

Neo-classical villa built for Walker Gray by John Nash 1798; privately owned until 1902 when acquired by local authority; converted for use as war hospital in 1916 and later incorporated into Royal Northern Hospital; occupied since 1985 by private clinic; fine grisaille panels representing classical scenes in Entrance Hall; handsome Staircase Hall; remarkable vaulted Breakfast Room painted to represent interior of aviary set in idyllic landscape. *(Pictured below)*

ROYAL HOSPITAL, CHELSEA

Address: Royal Hospital Road, SW3 4SL
Telephone: 0171 730 5282
Underground: Sloane Square
Open: 10am–12 noon–2–4pm Sun–Fri, 2–4pm Sat.

Hostel for disabled and veteran soldiers; founded by Charles II 1682; Grand Hall and Chapel designed by Sir Christopher Wren 1682–92; alterations to officers' apartments by Robert Adam 1765–92; minor buildings added by Sir John Soane; Hall and Chapel with fine woodwork and painted decoration; plain but handsome wards.

ST THOMAS'S OLD OPERATING THEATRE

Address: 9A St Thomas's Street, SE1 9RY

Underground: London Bridge
Admission: 12.30–4pm Mon, Wed, Fri.

Located in attic of chapter house of Southwark Cathedral; originally part of Guy's Hospital and used at one time as herb garret by house apothecary; converted for use as operating theatre 1821; unique example of its kind; gruesome but authentic.

SCHOOLS AND COLLEGES

HOME HOUSE

Address: 20 Portman Square, W1H 0BE
Underground: Bond Street

Neo-classical town house built 1773–6 for Dowager Countess of Home by Robert Adam; occupied from 1931 until 1992 by Courtauld Institute, art history faculty of the University of London founded by millionaire collector Samuel Courtauld; extremely well preserved; inlaid doors, marble chimney pieces, delicate plasterwork, painted panels by Angelica Kauffmann and Zucchi.

HARROW SCHOOL

Address: 1 High Street, Harrow-on-the-Hill, HA1 3HW
Telephone: 0181 422 2196
Underground: Harrow-on-the-Hill
Admission by prior arrangement.

School founded 1572 by John Lyon, local yeoman farmer; original building erected 1608–15 to provide assembly hall and class room (Fourth Form Room) for forty boys who originally made up school; Fourth Form Room more or less untouched, except for panelling, on which boys have been allowed to carve their names; graffiti by Byron, Sheridan, Trollope, Peel and Churchill; also of interest Speech Room and Vaughan Library.

RICHMOND FELLOWSHIP

Address: 8 Addison Road, W14 8DL
Underground: Holland Park
Admission by written application.

Peacock-coloured town house built for millionaire department store owner Sir Ernest Debenham, by Arts and Crafts architect, Halsey Ricardo; plasterwork by Ernest Gimson; stained glass by Edward Prior; woodwork by William Aumonier; glazed tiles by William de Morgan; interior, Principal Hall with mosaic ceiling added 1913 by Gaetano Meo and Byzantine-style stone carvings by George Jack; many other good rooms, notably Library, Drawing Room and Shower Room.

ST MARY'S COLLEGE

Address: Strawberry Hill, Waldegrave Road, Twickenham, TW1 5SX
Telephone: 0181 240 4000
Railway Station: Strawberry Hill
Admission by prior appointment.

Pioneering Gothic Revival villa originally occupied by wit and dilettante, Horace Walpole; begun c.1747; designed by 'Committee of Taste' presided over by Walpole himself and numbering among its members Richard Bentley and John Chute; Robert Adam at work in 1760s; office wing added 1779 by James Wyatt; Victorian wing added by chatelaine and amateur architect, Frances, Lady Waldegrave, 1860–2; most impressive interiors are Gallery, Holbein Bedroom, Library and Little Chapel.

ST PHILOMENA'S CONVENT

Address: Carshalton House, Pound Street, Carshalton, SN5 3PS
Telephone: 0181 642 2025
Railway Station: Carshalton
Admission: contact Sutton Library on 0181 770 4700 for details.

Built 1713 for Edward Carleton; acquired soon after by Dr John Radcliffe, physician to Queen Anne; converted for use as a school 1848; occupied since 1893 by St Philomena's Convent School; bathroom and water tower dating from 1719–20; original Painted Parlour with walls, doors and shutters depicting landscapes; fine woodwork in Blue Drawing Room, c.1750.

WESTMINSTER SCHOOL

Address: Ashburnham House, 6 Little Dean's Yard, SW1P 3PB
Telephone: 0171 963 1010
Underground: St James's Park
Open during Easter holidays.

Fifteenth-century Prior's lodging remodelled c.1662 for Willaim Ashburnham; acquired by Westminster School 1883; elegant Classical staircase attributed to John Webb (1611–72), pupil of Inigo Jones; also Cotton Library.

GOVERNMENT & CIVIC BUILDINGS

DEPTFORD TOWN HALL

Address: New Cross Road, SE14 6AE
Telephone: 0181 695 6000
Underground: New Cross
Admission by written application.

Built 1902–05 to designs of Charles E. Rickards; florid Baroque decoration on maritime theme highlighting Deptford's connections with Port of London; principal interiors and Staircase Hall.

FOREIGN & COMMONWEALTH OFFICE

Address: King Charles Street, SW1A 2AH
Telephone: 0171 270 1500
Underground: Westminster
Admission by written application.

Completed 1866; overall plan by George Gilbert Scott; many fine interiors, notably principal Staircase Hall, Foreign Secretary's Office, Council Chamber of India Office and Durbar Court; Durbar Court designed by Matthew Digby Wyatt with majolica friezes by Minton, Hollins & Co.

HOUSE OF LORDS

Address: Parliament Square, SW1A 0PW
Telephone: 0171 219 3000
Underground: Westminster
Admission: British nationals should apply in writing to their local M.P., foreign visitors should contact their embassy or consulate.

Built to designs of Sir Charles Barry, assisted by Augustus Pugin, 1840–70; occupies site of ancient Palace of Westminster, built for Edward the Confessor in mid-eleventh century and destroyed by fire 1834; tour de force of Gothic Revival architecture; majestic interior exhibiting work of the greatest artist-craftsmen.

LANCASTER HOUSE

Address: Stable Yard, St James's, SW1A 1BB
Underground: Green Park
Admission: 2–6pm Sat and Sun late Spring–early Autumn. The house may be closed at short notice for Government functions.

Begun 1825 for Frederick, Duke of York, second son of George III, to designs of Benjamin Wyatt; unfinished at time of York's death and purchased by Government; leased to Marquis of Stafford, later Duke of Sutherland; 1833–8 house completed under supervision of Sir Robert Smirke, architect of British Museum who added attic storey; Staircase Hall remodelled c.1838 by Sir Charles Barry, architect of Travellers' Club, Reform Club and House of Lords [q.v.]; house sold 1912 by Sutherlands heirs to Sir William Lever, who presented it to nation as centre for government hospitality; lavish Louis Revival and Italianate Palazzo style interiors in excellent state of preservation.

WESTMINSTER HALL

Address: Parliament Square, SW1A 0PW
Underground: Westminster

Built for Richard II by mason Henry Yevele and carpenter Hugh Herland, 1395–1403; stands on site of earlier hall built for William Rufus, 1097–99; scene of momentous events in English history, including trials of Sir Thomas More, Guy Fawkes and Charles II; restored by Sir Charles Barry after fire of 1834; survived both Blitz and more recent fire-bomb attack; interior little changed in almost 600 years; vast hammerbeam roof ornamented with angels bearing shields; stone carvings representing Kings of England.

....

LIVERY HALLS

WORSHIPFUL SOCIETY OF APOTHECARIES

Address: The Hall, Blackfriars Lane EC4V 6EJ
Telephone: 0171 236 1180
Underground: Blackfriars

Hall available for hire; occasional open days; apply in writing for details. Society granted charter by James I 1617; main block completed 1669–71 to designs of Thomas Locke with woodwork by Robert Byrges and Roger Davis; street front erected 1684 but extensively stuccoed 1786; minor alterations in nineteenth century; imposing hall with original reredos and panelling; unusual and finely wrought balustrade on main staircase; seventeenth- and eighteenth-century decoration in Court Room, Library and Parlour; fine collection of antique medicinal jars.

WORSHIPFUL COMPANY OF ARMOURERS AND BRAZIERS

Address: Armourers' Hall, 81 Coleman Street, EC2 5BJ
Telephone: 0171 606 1199
Underground: Bank

Company instituted 1322; granted livery company charter 1453; original pre-fire of London Hall pulled down 1840 and replaced by modest Neo-classical designed by T H Goode

WORSHIPFUL COMPANY OF DRAPERS

Address: Draper's Hall, EC2N 2DQ
Telephone: 0171 588 5001
Underground: Bank

Hall available for hire; occasional open days; apply in writing for details. Company established 1180; moved to present site 1541; original hall destroyed in Great Fire; much

subsequent rebuilding and redecoration; present structure dates in main from 1868–9 and was designed by Herbert Williams with decorative sculpture by E.W. Wyon; entrance front by Sir T.G. Jackson 1898–9; marble and alabaster Staircase Hall by same; magnificent Livery Hall with ceiling painted 1903–10 with allegories and scenes from Shakespeare; Court Drawing Room, 1869, with original furniture.

WORSHIPFUL COMPANY OF FISHMONGERS

Address: The Hall, London Bridge, EC4R 9EL
Telephone: 0171 626 3531
Underground: Monument
Three open days a year; apply in writing for details.

Company established thirteenth century; on or near present site since 1434; original hall destroyed in Great Fire; second hall pulled down 1827 to make way for London Bridge; present hall completed 1834 to designs of Henry Roberts assisted by George Gilbert Scott; restored 1929 by Goodhardt Rendel; damaged in Blitz and again restored by Austen Hall 1951; splendid Greek Revival interiors, particularly Entrance Hall, Staircase Hall, Banqueting Hall, Drawing Room and Court Room; many original furnishings.

WORSHIPFUL COMPANY OF STATIONERS AND NEWSPAPER MAKERS

Address: Stationer's Hall, Ave Maria Lane, EC4M 7DD
Telephone: 0171 248 2934
Underground: St Paul's
Hall available for hire, otherwise closed to visitors.

Stationers' guild formed 1403; granted livery company charter 1557; original hall destroyed in Great Fire; present building completed 1673, to designs of Stephen Colledge; street

Worshipful Company of Fishmongers

front refaced 1800 by Robert Mylne; new wing added 1887; damaged in Blitz and subsequently restored; original seventeenth-century panelling and carved oak screen in Hall, accompanied by late nineteenth-century stained glass windows on literary themes; seventeenth-century panelling and chimney-piece in Stock Room; original chimney-piece in Court Room.

....

The following list is of interiors which could not be included among the photographs in this book but which are of interest and open to the public.

BANQUETING HOUSE

Address: Whitehall, SW1A 2ER
Underground: Embankment
Telephone: 0171 930 4179
Open 10 am–5 pm Tues-Sat, Spring and Summer Bank Holiday, 2–5 pm Sun.

Majestic double cube interior by Inigo Jones with ceiling paintings by Rubens.

CARLYLE'S HOUSE

Address: 24 Cheyne Row, SW3 5HL
Telephone: 0171 352 7087
Underground: Sloane Square
Open 11 am–5 pm Wed-Sat and Bank Holiday Mon, Apr–Oct, 2–5 pm Sun Apr–Oct.

Terraced house of 1708 occupied by English historian Thomas Carlyle, 1834-81; well-preserved interior with many original features.

CHARTERHOUSE

Address: Charterhouse Square, EC1M 6AN
Telephone: 0171 253 9503
Underground: Barbican
Open 2.15–5 pm Wed, Apr–Jul.

Fourteenth-century Carthusian monastery converted into private house in the reign of Henry VIII and into almshouse and school in early seventeenth century; meticulously restored after bomb damage in Blitz; surviving Carthusian cloister and cell; sixteenth-century Great Hall.

CHISWICK HOUSE

Address: Burlington Lane, Chiswick W4 2RP
Telephone: 0181 995 0508
Underground: Turnham Green
Open 9.30 am–6.30 pm Mar–Oct, daily 9.30 am–4 pm Oct–Mar.

Model Palladian villa with surviving architectural decoration by William Kent and 3rd Earl of Burlington, *c.*1726–9

COLLEGE OF ARMS

Address: Queen Victoria Street, EC4V 4BT
Telephone: 0171 248 2762
Underground: Blackfriars or Mansion House
Open 10 am–4 pm Mon-Fri throughout year, except public holidays, state and special occasions.

Headquarters of England's heralds; building erected 1671–88; particularly impressive are Earl Marshal's Court (early eighteenth century) and adjoining Library (late seventeenth century).

CROSSNESS BEAM ENGINE HOUSE

Address: Belvedere Road, Thamesmead, DA2 9AQ
Railway Station: Abbey Wood, then Bus 272
Admission by prior appointment.

Outstanding Victorian ironwork and engineering structures.

CROYDON PALACE

Address: Old Palace Road, Croydon, Surrey CR0 1AX
Railway Station: West Croydon
Admission: apply in writing to The Secretary, Friends of Croydon Palace, at above address.

Former archbishop's palace with twelfth-century undercroft and surviving Hall built in reign of Henry VI.

DICKENS' HOUSE MUSEUM AND LIBRARY

Address: 48 Doughty Street, WC1N 2LF
Telephone: 0171 405 2127
Underground: Russell Square
Open 10 am–5 pm Mon-Sat.

Georgian terraced house occupied by novelist Charles Dickens 1837-9; some original furnishings, memorabilia.

DULWICH PICTURE GALLERY

Address: College Road, SE21 7AD
Telephone: 0181 693 8000
Railway Station: West Dulwich
Open 10 am–1 pm, 2–5 pm Tues-Sat, 2–5 pm Sun.

Oldest public art gallery in England; austere interiors by Sir John Soane, including mausoleum, 1811–4.

ELTHAM PALACE

Address: Eltham, SE9 5NR
Telephone: 0181 294 2548
Open 10 am–12 noon, 2.15–6 pm Thurs and Sun (Oct–4 Mar)

Former Royal Palace; Tudor Hall with hammerbeam roof , *c.*1480.

FENTON HOUSE

Address: Windmill Hill, NW3 6RT
Telephone: 0171 435 3471
Underground: Hampstead
Open 11 am–5 pm Sat and Sun, Mar.
Late seventeenth-century house with modest panelled interiors containing important collection of early keyboard instruments.

FORTY HALL MUSEUM

Address: Forty Hill, Enfield, EN2 9HA
Telephone: 0181 363 8169
Railway Station: Enfield Town, then Buses 231 or 191
Open 10 am–5 pm Tues–Sun, 1 Oct–Easter, 10 am–6 pm Tues–Sun, Easter–31 September.
Jacobean manor house built 1629-36, original carved screen in Hall; elaborate chimney-pieces and plasterwork.

GEFFRYE MUSEUM

Address: Kingsland Road, E2 8EA
Telephone: 0171 739 8368
Underground: Liverpool Street or Old Street
Open 10 am–5 pm Tues–Sat, 2–5 pm Sun, Bank Holiday Mon.
Early eighteenth-century alms-houses converted into museum of furniture and architectural decoration; reconstructions of English domestic interiors from Elizabethan times to the 1930s.

HAMPTON COURT PALACE

Address: East Molesley, Surrey, KT8 9AU
Telephone: 0181 781 9500
Railway Station: Hampton Court
Open 9.30 am–6 pm daily, 28 Mar–22 Oct, 9.30 am–4 pm daily, 23 Oct–27 Mar.
Begun early sixteenth century by Cardinal Wolsey; enlarged by Henry VIII after Wolsey's disgrace; largely completed by Sir Christopher Wren for William and Mary; early eighteenth-century addition by Sir John Vanbrugh and William Kent; state apartments opened to public by Queen Victoria 1838; surviving features from every phase of construction.

DOCTOR JOHNSON'S HOUSE

Address: 17 Gough Square, EC4 3DE
Telephone: 0171 353 3745
Underground: Chancery Lane
Open 11 am–5.30 pm Mon–Sat, 1 May–30 Sept, 11 am–5 pm Mon–Sat, 1 Oct–30 April.
Early Georgian town house occupied by man of letters, Samuel

Johnson, 1748–59; interiors restored in period.

KENSINGTON PALACE STATE APARTMENTS

Address: Kensington Gardens, W8 4PX
Telephone: 0171 937 9561
Underground: High Street Kensington
Open 9 am–5 pm Mon–Sat, 1–5 pm Sun, Bank Holidays.
Magnificent interiors ranging from reign of William and Mary to that of Queen Victoria.

KENWOOD HOUSE, IVEAGH BEQUEST

Address: Hampstead Lane, NW3 7JR
Telephone: 0181 348 1286
Underground: Golders Green or Highgate, then bus
Open 10 am–6 pm daily, 1 Apr–30 Sept, 10 am–4 pm daily, 1 Oct–31 Mar.
Fine Neo-classical interiors by Robert Adam dating from 1760s; important collection of pictures and furniture.

KEW PALACE

Address: Kew, Richmond, Surrey, TW9 3AB
Telephone: 0171 940 3321
Underground: Kew
Open 11 am–5.30 pm daily, 1 Apr–30 Sept.
Seventeenth-century gabled house remodelled in eighteenth century as suburban retreat for George III and Queen Charlotte; modest but distinguished interiors.

MIDDLE TEMPLE HALL

Address: Middle Temple Lane, EC4Y 9AT
Telephone: 0171 427 4800
Underground: Temple
Open 10–11.30 am, 3–4 pm Mon–Fri, except August.
Hall built 1562–70; original carved screen and double hammerbeam roof.

NATURAL HISTORY MUSEUM

Address: Cromwell Road, South Kensington, SW7 5BD
Telephone: 0171 589 6323
Underground: South Kensington
Open 10 am–6 pm Mon–Sat, 11 am–6 pm Sun.
Breathtaking late nineteenth-century interiors by Alfred Waterhouse.

NATIONAL MARITIME MUSEUM

Address: Romney Road, Greenwich, SE10 9NF
Telephone: 0181 858 4422
Railway Station: Greenwich
Open 10 am–6 pm Mon–Sat, 12 noon–6 pm Sun, 1 Apr–30 Sept; 10 am–5 pm Mon–Sat, 12 noon–5 pm Sun, 1 Oct–31 Mar.
Incorporating Queen's House with Palladian interiors by John Webb, pupil of Inigo Jones, 1664–9; Royal Naval College with early eighteenth-century dining hall by Wren (assisted by Nicholas Hawksmoor) decorated with allegorical wall and ceiling paintings by Sir James Thornhill, early Greek Revival Chapel by James 'Athenian' Stuart 1780-8.

PITSHANGER MANOR MUSEUM

Address: Mattock Lane, Ealing, W5 5EQ
Telephone: 0181 567 1227
Underground: Ealing Broadway
Admission: Telephone for details;
Neo-classical villa with surviving decoration by George Dance (Drawing Room and Eating Room of 1768) and Sir John Soane (Breakfast Room of *c.*1803)

RED HOUSE

Address: 13 Red House Lane, Bexleyheath, Kent, DA6 8JF
Railway Station: Bexleyheath
Open one weekday each month, apply in writing.
Arts and Crafts interiors by William Morris and Philip Webb, *c.*1860

SWAKELEY'S HOUSE

Address: The Avenue, Ickenham, Middlesex
Underground: Ickenham
Open 3 days a year, apply for details.
Jacobean manor house built in 1629–38; original carved screen in Hall; Staircase compartment frescoed with scenes from antiquity.

SYON HOUSE

Address: Syon Park, London Road, Brentford, TW8 8JF
Underground: Gunnersbury, then buses 237 or 267
Open 12 noon–5 pm Sun–Thurs, Apr–Aug.
Fifteenth-century convent remodelled in mid-eighteenth century by Robert Adam; sumptuous Neo-classical interiors.

VICTORIA AND ALBERT MUSEUM

Address: Cromwell Road, SW7 2RL
Telephone: 0171 589 6371
Underground: South Kensington
Open 10 am–5.30 pm Mon-Thurs and Sat, 12 noon–5.50 pm Sun.
Many fine interiors, including William Morris Rooms.

WELLINGTON MUSEUM

Address: Apsley House, 149 Piccadilly, W1V 9FA
Telephone: 0171 499 5676
Underground: Hyde Park Corner
Open 11 am–5 pm Tues–Sun. Bank Holidays (except May Day).
London home of 1st Duke of Wellington 1817-52; Neo-classical interiors by Robert Adam; 'Louis XIV' interiors by Benjamin Wyatt; superb collection of porcelain.

INDEX